THE UNDISCOVERED ARC[...]
LANDSCAPE IN AND AROUN[...]
WOODALL, SOUTH Y[...]

By Paul Rowland

"Harthill is probably the least well documented area of the whole of the Rotherham Metropolitan Borough, and the museum only gets to know about finds etc., if they are reported to the museum. It is not because there is no archaeology in the Harthill and Loscar Farm area, it is simply because people choose not to disclose their finds, and as such it has never been brought to the attention of Rotherham Museum nor the SYAS before. That is why the SYAS and Rotherham Museum has so little information about the area surrounding Harthill and the Loscar Farm Area."

Karl Noble, Heritage Assistant, Rotherham Museum

"There has been very little previous archaeological work within and around Harthill..."

Archaeological Watching Brief, North Cottage, 4 Union Street, Harthill, Rotherham, South Yorkshire. Wessex Archaeology. July 2013.

CONTENTS

INTRODUCTION

Since 1987, when I first came to live in the village of Harthill with Woodall, the history of the village and the surrounding landscape has fascinated me and I have researched and studied its history at length.

The pages that follow are reports that I was asked to write as part of the *Harthill Action Group*, a local village group that was formed in opposition to the Loscar Wind Farm development at Loscar Farm in 2005.

At the time, I did wonder what evidence that I, as an amateur, but *enthusiastic* local historian could come up with when faced with the archaeological assessment written by Npower Renewables professional archaeologists, Oxford Archaeology North.

My fears were soon dismissed after reading OAN's first archaeological report. They had made lots of false assumptions and had not looked at any locally written or oral histories about the area. I did wonder at the time whether their report had been written by a 15 year old as it was so poorly researched and written.

OAN admitted that Packman Lane was probably an ancient road but they totally dismissed it as ever being a Roman road because it *"lacks the linearity, regularity and continuity that is typical of Roman roads."* They then stated in their report that the main road through the village itself was more likely to have been a Roman road because it *"includes a long linear stretch, which is also a possible candidate for the route of a Roman road."* that is despite the fact that there has never been any suggestion written, oral or other that has ever stated that it ever was a Roman road.

"The townships of Harthill and Thorpe Salvin, and, in that quarter, the honours of Coningsborough and Tickhill, are separated by a narrow road, proceeding in a straight line, called in some early writings a Roman road. These townships are at the most southern point of the whole county, and where the road enters the county is Streethouses, a name which is rarely found except on the line of a Roman road. Again, Thorpe Salvin is often called in antient authorities Rykenildthorpe [after the Roman road, Ryknild Street.]¹. All these circumstances concur remarkably in fixing upon this antient highway the character of remote and even Roman or British antiquity. Further, pieces of Roman money are picked up from time to time near its course." Joseph Hunter, *'Hunter's Archaeological Survey of South Yorkshire.'* 2 Vols. Published 1828-1831.

As I said earlier, I am no archaeological expert, although I have studied Landscape Archaeology and studied for a Masters degree in Imperialism & Culture.

---

[1] Ryknild Street was a branch of the Fosse Way (which ran from Exeter to nearby Lincoln) and ran from Bourton on the Water in the Cotswolds to Rotherham via Birmingham. A substantial highway that must surely have promoted a lot of settlement along its route.

I am just an amateur, local historian and researcher. However, I have spent most of my life researching history and for over 20 years wrote, edited and published a genealogical and history magazine. I have been commissioned to write articles for history magazines, including Burkes' Peerage online journal, appeared on several UK radio stations talking about history and even carried out genealogical research for three episodes of the BBC's award winning TV programme, *'Who Do You Think You Are'* for the impersonator, Alisair McGowan, the actor, Rupert Penry-Jones and the comedian, Billy Connolly. Look for my name on the end credits of those episodes.

The information that I am putting before you here, (which was originally written to stop the destruction of Harthill's archaeological features and hedgerows during the Loscar Wind Farm development) are the details showing evidence of *possible* archaeological features in and around Harthill that I have come across over the years, plus information I have been given by local residents.

The continual industrialisation of Britain's Green Belt land is deeply worrying for all of us and for future generations. Loscar Common is within the Green Belt and is a designated an Area of High Landscape Value (AHLV). Rotherham's Unitary Development Plan (UDP) affords this area a very high level of protection and any development within it has to prove *Very Special Circumstances.* Sadly, the wind farm development opened the back door to the further industrialisation of Green Belt land at Loscar and the recent proposal in 2017 by INEOS to carry out *Shale Gas Fracking* at Loscar on land adjacent to Common Road, Harthill is sadly further proof of this.

One can only hope that this document may stir someone or some organisation with the resources and the professional knowledge to look closer at the *possible* archaeological features in and around Harthill with Woodall that I have outlined here before it is too late and they are lost forever.

HARTHILL ACTION GROUP.

Response to:

Loscar Farm Wind Turbines Proposed Development.

Report compiled by The Energy Workshop Ltd for John Wilks.

ARCHAEOLOGICAL ASSESSMENT. PART 2.

By Paul Rowland.

SUMMARY

This report by Harthill Action Group is a response to the archaeological assessment undertaken by Oxford Archaeology North, on behalf of Npower Renewables.

INTRODUCTION

In the short period of time available to us to respond to the archaeological assessment we have also undertaken a desk-based assessment, using primary and secondary sources, local knowledge and aerial photography. We also held discussions about the proposed site with the following organisations.

- South Yorkshire Sites and Monuments Records. Jim McNeil, Sites and Monuments Officer.

- Derbyshire Record Office. Jill Stroud, Sites and Monuments Officer.

- Yorkshire Archaeological Society. Alan Betteridge, Archivist.

- Sheffield Archives.

- Rotherham Museum.

- Sheffield Local Studies Library.

- Sheffield Museum.

- Sheffield City Council. Gaynor Boon, Ecologist/ Environmentalist.

- Cresswell Heritage Trust. Ian Wall, Archaeologist.

- Alan Hall, Archaeologist.

- Sheffield University – Hunter Archaeological Society.

INTRODUCTION

I have read the two archaeological assessment reports submitted by Npower Renewables with regard to their proposed wind turbine development at Loscar Farm, Harthill.

The first report arrogantly chose to ignore many well-known sources that they could have easily searched for details about the history of this area. Their attempts at field walking when the field was in crop, quite frankly, beggared belief, and their report was nothing more than a whitewash that chose to ignore several sites and factors all of which I pointed out in my report.

Npower's second report is simply a rewording of their first report with the exception that more fields were examined by field walking and a wide variety of finds, covering a broad period in time were discovered.

Their second report also limited the *'other sites of special interest'* surrounding the proposed site at Loscar Farm to within 1km of the site. This of course, 'conveniently ignores several key sites surrounding Loscar Farm which have a direct relevance to Packman Lane, such as the Roman road from Markland Grips which Derbyshire SMR suggests linked up with Packman Lane. It also ignores the enclosures and Roman archaeological finds at Whitwell Wood.

HEDGEROWS

The second report also totally ignores the issue of the removal of the hedgerows along Packman Lane. In their first report,

Npower identified 7 different species of trees growing in the hedgerows. In archaeological terms, using a technique known as Hooper's Hypothesis, one species of tree denotes a period of one hundred years, so Npower confirmed that the hedgerows along Packman Lane were approximately 700 years old! Interesting then, that their second report chooses to completely ignore the hedgerows along Packman Lane. Could this be because their chosen route to the site at Loscar Farm, at the southern end of Packman Lane, is via the northern end of Packman Lane. This will of course mean the large scale removal of long stretches of hedgerows and trees along the route. Npower only briefly allude to this in their reports, but state that the road will need widening from 3 metres to 6 metres; it will require strengthening and realigning for their huge lorries and machinery to access the site.

As part of my ongoing research into the area around the proposed wind farm site at Loscar Farm I have looked at several maps of the area, all of different dates to ascertain whether or not it can be proven that Packman Lane was in fact a Roman road.

I personally believe that Packman Lane predates the Romans by several centuries and was probably a prehistoric ridgeway that was later pressed into service by the Romans. This makes it even more precious and worth fighting to save from destruction.

I have spoken to local farmers and older local villagers who can attest to the fact that Roman coins have been found along Packman Lane, some of which are recorded in the South Yorkshire Sites and Monuments Records and Clifton Park Museum, Rotherham. An impressive collection of Roman coins found on Carr Farm land is still in the possession of the farmer, Mr Alan Skepper and can be seen at the end of this report. The discovery of Roman coins proves that Packman Lane and the land between it and the current day village of Harthill was frequented by the Romans.

Looking at the different maps and aerial photographs of the area around Loscar I have noticed a couple of interesting things.

1. Due south of Loscar Farm is the Romano-British camp at Markland Grips.

2. Due north of Loscar Farm at Thurcroft is another Roman camp.

Drawing a point between the two sites produces a line that runs almost vertically along Packman Lane![2]

Almost half way between these two sites, (4 miles apart) a dark rectangular feature can be seen on aerial photographs. The feature is situated on Packman Lane, just north of the crossroads between Harthill and Thorpe Salvin heading towards Kiveton Park.

I have looked at the different maps of the area to see whether this could be a former field boundary, but none of the maps shows a field boundary in this position.

---

[2] *Since I wrote this report, Mr John Fisher, a local historian from North Anston gave me a copy of an archaeological excavation report produced by 'The Hunter Archaeological Society' Vol. IX, Part 3., dated 1967, which shows that there was another Roman camp closer to Harthill situated behind 'The Station Pub' at Kiveton Park at the end of current northern end of Packman Lane.*

I also spoke to a farmer whose family previously owned the field and he confirmed that there was never a field boundary in that area. This rectangular feature could have been a staging post between the two Roman sites (north and south) or it could be a Roman settlement guarding the crossroads. However, whatever the rectangular mark is, it warrants further investigation prior to any consent for road widening, realignment and road strengthening is allowed to go ahead.

Npower state that Packman Lane is of great antiquity but state that its age cannot be proven. But they are prepared to dig it up and alter it beyond recognition without carrying out any archaeological surveys and excavations along it before they destroy it forever.

Npower claim that Packman Lane was never a Roman road. The RMBC should make Npower carry out a full archaeological survey and carry out excavations along Packman Lane to disprove or prove their theory once and for all.

Both the South Yorkshire and Derbyshire SMR confirmed that there has never been an archaeological dig along Packman Lane. Now is the time to change that! The RMBC cannot allow Packman Lane to be destroyed without a thorough independent archaeological survey being carried out first.

Rotherham Metropolitan Borough Council must ensure that Npower are not allowed to damage this ancient lane. Packman Lane has carried people along it since prehistoric times. Npower's archaeological finds have proven this by the wide date range of items found around it. To allow it to be dug up after almost a millennia, and changed into a dual carriageway for the benefit of Npower shareholders will be something that the RMBC, along with the local community must fight to stop.

Like Npower, I have nothing to add to my original report. Npower have clearly not proven beyond a reasonable doubt that the age and importance of Packman Lane is not worthy of a full archaeological survey and excavation. By choosing not to carry out a full archaeological survey along the length of Packman Lane Npower are again acting arrogantly towards the

RMBC and the local community. Npower know that once an archaeological dig is allowed to be carried out along Packman Lane, then the antiquity and importance of Packman Lane will stand in the way of shareholders profits. That is the reason why they do not want a survey and excavation to be undertaken along it. And, that is why they have chosen to ignore it.

RESPONSE TO OAN's METHODOLOGY

In their archaeological assessment, OAN state that their desk-based assessment of the land around the proposed site;

"...had been in agricultural use since at least the sixteenth century, with field names remaining largely unchanged for centuries. The eastern edge of the study area coincides with what was undoubtedly an ancient road, but its precise antiquity is unknown. Much of the land within the study area comprises shaped field strip fields that are a product of the enclosure of medieval open fields, and are documented as being within the manorial estate of Harthill. The Honeysyke Farm is a post-

medieval farm and the adjacent Loscar Farm was built in the early twentieth century."

Because the land was *'first'* Recorded as being in use from at least the sixteenth century, does not mean that the land was not in use before then. A look at some of the recorded finds at the South Yorkshire Sites and Monuments Records shows that they have records of at least two finds earlier than the 16th century. These were found just north of Loscar Farm land, only one of which has been noted by the OAN; (SMR No. 3455 – Early Medieval Strap End, dating from the 10th century). The other item unrecorded by the OAN is: (SMR No. 3456 – Early Medieval Strap End, dating from the 9th century). Why is there no mention of this other find? In the SMR records it comes immediately after the find (3455) that the OAN have noted? If they had carried out *'proper'* and *'thorough'* research into this area shouldn't item 3456 have been noted also? It is of no more or lesser importance than item 3455 which they did record?

The OAN have obviously consulted primary sources and maps of the area, some of which they have noted in their report. However, considering the implications that the proposed wind turbines would have on the local community and the area in general, I would have hoped that their report would have been more than just cursory. The OAN admit that their report consisted of a *"rapid desk-based study"* (Environmental Statement – Addendum. p.5. 2.1.2).

THE DUKES OF LEEDS ARCHIVE

I was surprised to see the omission of the name of the Yorkshire Archaeological Society from the OAN's list of sources searched considering that the Yorkshire Archaeological Society holds the Dukes of Leeds massive archive. The Dukes of Leeds were the largest landowner in and around Harthill from the 1600s up to the 20th century!

SHEFFIELD UNIVERSITY – HUNTER ARCHAEOLOGICAL SOCIETY

I was also very surprised to see that the OAN had not even contacted the Hunter Archaeological Society at Sheffield

University, nor consulted Hunter's two volume publication, simply titled; *"South Yorkshire by Hunter"* Volume 1., being published in 1828, the second in 1831. This contains a very indepth account of the history of Harthill and the wider surrounding area. It should have been one of the most obvious sources for them to have used.

If their research into this area was unable to identify this well-known and important reference work, then its shows ineptitude of the highest calibre. However, if they did identify it in their research and chose to ignore it then it shows their arrogance and complete lack of respect for the people of Harthill, Rotherham Borough Council and the people of Rotherham.

If they were indeed serious about researching the archaeological evidence at Loscar Farm and the surrounding area, as they would like us to believe, then they could have accessed Sheffield University's website without leaving their desks!

The following information is taken directly from Sheffield

University's own website: *"The Hunter Archaeological Society was founded in 1912 to study and report on the archaeology, history and architecture of South Yorkshire and North Derbyshire.*

The Society is named after Joseph Hunter (1783-1861) who is, perhaps, best known locally for his publications "Hallamshire" (1819) and the two volumes of "South Yorkshire" (1828 & 1831). They form indispensable sources of reference for all historians of the county.

He was born on 6 February 1783 in Sheffield, the son of a cutler. Educated at Attercliffe, he later studied theology at New College in York, becoming a Unitarian Minister in Bath in 1809.

He never again lived in South Yorkshire though often returned in the course of his researches into the area.

His early interest in antiquarian studies covered a wide field and this interest became his professional career when, in 1833, he was appointed a sub-commissioner of the Records

Commission and moved to London. In 1838 he became an Assistant Keeper of the Public Records and is particularly remembered for his work in classifying the Exchequer records. He was Vice-President of the Society of Antiquaries."

(http://www.shef.ac.uk/archaeology/hunter/society.html).

WALK-OVER SURVEY

In their summary, the OAN also makes a surprising admission about their walk-over survey of the proposed site for the wind turbines. They state;

"The walk-over survey was not productive as most of the fields containing locations for the proposed wind turbines were under crop. No archaeological remains were identified, and the lack of surface survival in part reflects that the land has been subject to repeated ploughing."

The fact that they attempted a walk-over survey of the proposed site to record and assess the suitability of that site for National Wind Power Ltd., whilst the crops in the fields were;

"up to waist height." (Environmental Statement – Addendum. p.6. 2.3.3) is, quite frankly, worrying! Even someone with little knowledge of the subject but with a modicum of common sense would know that a field walk under those conditions would only ever discover what they were hoping they would find…Nothing! Why were no more surveys undertaken at different times of the year, when a *'proper'* and thorough survey could have been undertaken?

I have studied Landscape Archaeology and I am disappointed that an august body, such as the OAN has not given this site anything more that a cursory look. They should have been looking for 'any' evidence that would suggest that the proposed site was suitable or unsuitable for National Wind Power's wind turbines at Loscar. As such, one cannot believe or trust the findings of their evidence. With regard to National Wind Power's archaeological assessment, their *'walk-over survey'* is, we feel, an attempt to try and *'walk-over'* the local community and Rotherham Borough Council!

The OAN also state; *"Where possible, photographs were taken in black and white print and colour slide from the edge of the fields showing the proposed position of the wind turbines."*

In an archaeological assessment of the land where wind turbines or any other large structures are proposed, It is vitally important, both locally and nationally to be content that *'proper'* research has been undertaken to preserve our heritage *'prior'* to development, after which it would be far too late.

What use are photographs taken from the edge of the field when they should have been looking at the land beneath their feet? Were they gathering archaeological evidence or producing a calendar! Why did they not at least dig a 1 metre test ditch on Mr Wilks' land in an attempt to at least *'try'* and discover any archaeological evidence? They are archaeologists after all… that is what they are supposed to do, is it not?

Again, one questions the validity of their findings in their report. Anyone who has ever watched Channel Four's archaeological programme, *'Time Team'* on television would be left scratching their heads wondering where is the Geophysical Survey of the site? Why are there no aerial photographs which could possibly highlight areas of importance around the site? There is an airfield at Thorpe Salvin where a plane could have been hired for under £40.00 for a 30 minute flight to take photographs of the site. Was the OAN's *'walk-over survey'* assessment carried out by professionals or amateurs?

Another statement by the OAN does make one wonder if they have any knowledge of the depth that the foundations of wind turbines are dug to!

"On the present evidence it is suggested that the proposed wind farm will impact on fields where no archaeology has been positively identified; but where there exists a potential for the survival of below ground remains."

Npower state in their planning application that 641 cubic metres of soil, rock and stone will be removed to construct the foundations of *each* wind turbine. At that depth of 3 metres, the *'potential'* for the survival of below ground archaeological remains, that may currently lie hidden, will be lost forever!

The OAN also state that; *"Had a site of archaeological potential been identified the extent of it would have been defined if greater than 50m in size, anything less would have been recorded as a central point only."*

This statement is baffling, and is again, worrying because Packman Lane, the road on which Loscar Farm is situated and along which NPower's lorries will have to travel to their proposed site is recorded as being a Roman road and is well over 50m in length, but it has not been recorded by the OAN, even though they admit in their summary that Packman Lane; *"was undoubtedly an ancient road, but its precise antiquity is unknown."*

Surely, the *'precise antiquity'* of Packman Lane is one of, if not *THE* most important things that OAN were employed by Npower to discover?

The fact that the OAN have chosen to simply disregard Packman Lane with a cursory remark, does make one wonder why? Was it because this would involve time and money and the possibility that they *would* discover sizeable archaeological evidence on Packman Lane? Or, was it because they were unable to find a convenient *'documented'* record about it?

The fact that they have chosen *not* to investigate Packman Lane, the single stretch of road alongside National Wind Power's proposed site is quite frankly beyond comprehension! By not investigating the *'precise antiquity'* of Packman Lane it proves that the OAN have *NOT* undertaken a thorough investigation of the site around Loscar Farm and the surrounding area, and their report should be viewed with extreme caution.

OAN SOURCES

The OAN in their Methodology, on page 5 state that they have... *"an extensive library of secondary sources relevant to the study area, as well as numerous unpublished client reports on work carried out under its former title of Lancaster University Archaeological Unit (LUAU) and as OA North. These were also consulted where necessary."*

This statement is rather ambiguous! Are these *'secondary sources'* listed in their bibliography?

In their bibliography they cite a source they have consulted; Newbold, P. 1999-2003 Keveton/Keeton Hall (1698-1811) http://www.j31.co.uk/kivhall.html.

This consists of nothing more than a single amateur web page with four small paragraphs about Kiveton Hall! Surely, if they were looking for *'proper'* background information about Kiveton Hall they should have consulted the following work; Twibell, Arthur. 1989. *Kiveton Hall: A Study in South Yorkshire,* WEA Yorkshire District (South). 34 pages!

ARCHAEOLOGICAL SITES IN THE VICINITY

On page 6, of their Environmental Statement – Addendum. 2.4 Gazetteer of Sites, the OAN state that; *"All of the information concerning archaeological sites in the vicinity of the development site has been collated into a gazetteer (Appendix*

2), which provides details of their location, origin, and character...”

2.4.2. “ Other sites beyond the extent of the study area, which were considered to be of background relevance, are mentioned in the text with appropriate SMR references.”

Considering the fact that the southern most portion of Mr Wilks' land at Loscar is on the boundary of South Yorkshire and North Derbyshire and is separated by Bondhay Dyke, one would expect the OAN to have consulted the Derbyshire Records Office to search the Sites and Monuments Records for North Derbyshire. However, in a telephone conversation with Jill Stroud, the Sites and Monuments Officer at Derbyshire Records Office on Thursday, November 18th 2004. She told me that she was *“surprised”* that she had *NOT* been approached by OAN or Npower in relation to the proposed wind turbine development at Loscar Farm.

This shows the arrogance of both Npower and the OAN towards the local community and Rotherham Borough Council. The fact that they did not even deem it necessary to contact the

Derbyshire Record Office to speak to the Sites and Monuments Officer speaks volumes about Npower and their proposed development at Loscar Farm, and highlights the shortcomings of the OAN's report.

The Bondhay Dyke which runs along the boundary of South Yorkshire and North Derbyshire, was, in fact, once the *'natural'* boundary between the lands of Mercia and Northumbria. Harthill was situated in Northumbria and the neighbouring village of Whitwell was situated in Mercia.

WHITWELL

The location of the neighbouring village of Whitwell is of major importance, considering its proximity to the proposed site, and yet the OAN do not even mention it or acknowledge its importance by showing that they have even consulted anything about it in their sources.

Whitwell was first mentioned in the Anglo-Saxon Chronicles in 942 AD. Professor Dorothy Whitelock, a universally respected Anglo-Saxonist translated the following:

"In this year King Edmund, lord of the English, protector of men, the beloved performer of mighty deeds, overran Mercia, as bounded by Dore, Whitwell gate, and the broad stream, the River Humber; and five boroughs, Leicester and Lincoln, Nottingham and likewise Stamford, and also Derby." (Peters, Capt. R. J. *The Ancient Villages of Whitwell and Barlborough: with a study of the Celtic and Anglo-Saxon Boundaries of the Region.* General Editor: R. J. Peters. 1990, North Trent Publishing, Sutton-in-Ashfield, Notts).

The boundary between Harthill and Whitwell Gate was obviously a boundary of considerable importance. But the OAN do not make any reference to it, even though they state; *"All of the information concerning archaeological sites in the vicinity of the development site has been collated..."* Except for the important neighbouring archaeological sites at Whitwell, Clowne, Markland Grips, Cresswell, Barlborough and most importantly; Packman Lane, Harthill!

In reality, it would appear that the OAN have not looked much further than the boundaries of the proposed site and certainly no further than the end of their noses!

In the book; *'The Ancient Villages of Whitwell and Barlborough: with a study of the Celtic and Anglo-Saxon Boundaries of the Region.'* General Editor: R.J. Peters. 1990, North Trent Publishing, Sutton-in-Ashfield, Notts. Captain Roy Peters says; *"Parish boundaries do, to a great extent, reflect the boundaries of medieval estates. Thus the further back one goes into history then the more does the history of a village become the history of a single estate, about which very little can be known.* ***More and more the historian needs to look at the district, the area, the region, in order to throw light upon that single small estate...*** *We start by using a floodlight rather than a searchlight in order to illuminate an area considerably larger than the village. Only later do we collimate that floodlight into a searchlight and focus upon the village itself."*

Captain Peters continues; *"This process of working from the general to the particular – the process known to logic as 'deduction'...*" is something that the OAN appear to be devoid of!

The OAN's archaeological research into the site area around Loscar Farm is not of an adequate, satisfactory or even of a professional standard, that one would have hoped and expected it to have been. If their assessment is to be even considered as valid and worthy of note in this case, then the site area around Loscar Farm and the wider surrounding area requires much more than a cursory glance and as such one wonders how anyone can trust the findings of their archaeological assessment of the site area around Loscar Farm?

Sites such as Whitwell, Clowne, Barlborough and Cresswell also need to be researched by the OAN if they are truly serious in asking us all to accept the findings of their archaeological assessment of the Loscar Farm area as being adequately and thoroughly researched.

ROMAN & ROMANO-BRITISH PERIOD

"Within and around Whitwell a number of Roman finds have

been discovered, and both Markland Grips promontory fort and Cresswell Crags have shown evidence of Roman and Romano-British occupation. The enclosure near Barlborough, a quarter mile south of Carr Plantation, is Romano-British, with signs of later use." (Capt. R.J. Peters, p.55). neither of these two sites have been mentioned in the OAN's archaeological assessment. Why is that?

In a telephone conversation with Ian Wall, the archaeologist at Cresswell Heritage Trust, on Friday 19th November 2004, I asked if they had any records of Roman occupation in the area near to Loscar Farm. He confirmed that a well documented Roman horde was discovered in two jars at Whitwell in 1850. And another Roman horde was discovered on the road below Clowne to Dansbruck. The OAN makes no mention of these archaeological finds. Why is that, if they were truly recording *"All of the information concerning archaeological sites in the vicinity of the development site…"?*

MARKLAND GRIPS

In a telephone conversation with Jill Stroud, Sites and

Monuments Officer at Derbyshire Record Office on Thursday 18th November 2004, I asked her if she had any archaeological documents or surveys relating to Markland Grips. She said that on their maps; *"their is a suggested Roman road running from Markland Grips from Clowne down Gapsick Lane along Gypsy Hill Lane."* This may be of interest for the OAN to note, because if you head north from Markland Grips along the Derbyshire Records *'suggested'* Roman road, down Gapstick Lane and along Gypsy Hill Lane the road continues north along Bondhay Common, crosses Bondhay Dyke *(the South Yorkshire, North Derbyshire county boundary)* and joins up with Packman Lane, Harthill!

"One element related to the importance of Packman Road as a route is the presence, within about half a mile, of the ancient Promontory Fort of Markland Grips. In Celtic, Roman, and Anglo-Saxon times it guarded this part of the boundary." (Captain R.J. Peters. P.27).

Captain Roy Peters also states in his book;

"We know that at one point in history the boundary between Mercia [North Derbyshire] and Northumbria [South Yorkshire] passed through or close to Whitwell. There is evidence that Whitwell might also have been on the boundary over a hundred years earlier than that single historical record tells us. But when we look at other evidence, such as the military fortifications near the boundary, the structure of Celtic states in the area and their probable continuity as Civitas during Roman rule, the structure of Anglo-Saxon states in the area, and the form of the modern boundary, then one is left with the inescapable conclusion that the boundary of which Whitwell (certainly) and Barlborough (virtually certainly) formed a part is one which probably has had a continuous existence for at least two milenia."

This would suggest that Packman Lane and the land around Loscar was almost certainly of major strategic importance even before Roman times. Its continued strategic importance is also borne out by the fact that the Romans occupied the promontory fort a short distance away at Markland Grips. Again, why is there is no mention of this site within the report of the OAN?

"The promontory fort of Markland Grips held a position of special importance because it was on a 'triple point' where the three kingdoms of the Brigantes, the Cornavii, and the Coritani met. It also commanded the passing of the Packman Road, which itself ran southwards roughly along the boundary between the latter two kingdoms." (Capt. R. J. Peters. P.55).

PACKMAN LANE

"Undoubtedly the Romans adapted and used our Packman Road, before they set about building Ricknield Street through Chesterfield and Eckington. (confusingly, parts of Packman Road subsequently became known as Ricknield Street, perhaps because it was linked at some point to the 'true' Roman road)." (Capt. R.J. Peters. P.55).

Captain Peters remark that Packman Lane probably linked up *"at some point to the 'true' Roman road of Ricknield Street,"* is probably correct. Packman Lane was situated at a very important strategic point as mentioned earlier and was probably in use from prehistoric times.

There were at least three different types of Roman roads that I am aware of; the most well known ones were built as imperial highways to carry messages *"and for the rapid movement of troops; they were furnished with posting stations with relays of horses about every 10 miles and with lodging places (mansions) about every 25 miles. These roads were the '**via publicae regales'**. Where possible they took the direct line between towns, marshy ground being crossed by using piles and embankments, and cuttings and even tunnels being constructed in hilly country. A network of smaller roads (**viae vicinales**) linked up the smaller towns and there were also recognised earth tracks (**viae terrenae**).* (Encyclopaedia Britannica. Vol. 19. P.340, 1959, London).

Without further investigation we will never know which category of road Packman Lane was in Roman times. And, if Captain Peters suggestion is correct that Packman Lane probably predates the *'true'* Ricknield Street as a Roman road, why have the OAN chosen to totally dismiss Packman Lane as a site worthy of further investigation?

An even more fatuous remark by the OAN in their archaeological assessment about Packman Lane that highlights the crass level of the research undertaken, and the alarming level of ineptitude by them is contained in the following paragraph; [a] *"The line of Packman Lane was clearly remote from the line of the road known to extend through Chesterfield; in any case the line of Packman Lane lacks the linearity, regularity and continuity that is typical of Roman roads and yet which is clearly evident on the line of Ryknild Street to the south of Chesterfield."* [b] *"The only evidence for it having been a Roman road would appear to be the linking of the name Rykenild (sic) Street to this stretch of road. In addition to these roads, the road immediately west of Packman Lane, which passes through Harthill, includes a long linear stretch, which is also a possible candidate for the route of a Roman road."* [c] *"Considering the strong evidence for the Roman roads to the west of Packman Lane, and the lack of linearity of Packman Lane itself, it is considered that Packman Lane was firstly not on the line of Ryknild Roman road and was probably unlikely to be a Roman road."*

This paragraph requires a three-fold response. [a] *"In most cases road alignments were laid out by surveyors from one hilltop to another. These sighting points would be mutually visible, possibly with the aid of fires and beacons.*

Intermediate points of the same line could be laid out easily on lower ground, <u>not necessarily dead straight</u> as more useful purposes could sometimes be served by slight deviations to avoid natural obstacles, or even man-made ones like burial mounds. To descend escarpments or cross rivers it was permissible to zig zag and dig terraceways or make cuttings as required by the nature of the locality rather than stick to the rigid straight line. Steep gradients up to 1 in 6 and fording rivers were not deterrents.

Considering the desire to keep their roads on high ground as far as practicable, it is not surprising that many ridgeways,

41

Neolithic routes and iron-age trackways were pressed into service perhaps late in the 1st century A.D. and Romanised." (Bagshawe, Richard W. *Notes to Roman Roads.* 1979, Shire Publications Ltd.)

[b] The suggestion by the OAN that the road through the village of Harthill itself is a *"possible candidate for the route of a Roman road,"* is, quite frankly staggering! But at the same time it is remarkably convenient for Npower. Archaeologists and historians rely on physical, documentary and oral evidence to unravel the mysteries of the past. And, whilst there is plenty of evidence to suggest that Packman Lane was used by the Romans, and probably even pre-dates them by several centuries, there is absolutely no physical, documentary or oral evidence whatsoever to suggest that the road through Harthill village is a more likely candidate to be a Roman road simply because *"it includes a long linear stretch."!!*

I spoke to two archaeologists that I know about this statement, Ian Wall, Archaeologist at Cresswell Heritage Trust and Alan

Hall, an archaeologist friend who until recently worked for Sheffield Museum. Both laughed at the OAN's ridiculous statement and suggested that the OAN were naïve to believe that all Roman roads were straight!

Although the OAN have listed in its bibliography the following book; *'Garbett, H. 1950. The History of Harthill-w-Woodall and its hamlet Kiveton Park (the latter until AD 1868 when it becomes part of Wales parish), Ilfracombe, North Devon.'* It is obvious that they have not read it, because Garbett records an oral account by a parishoner of Harthill known as 'Cobbler Storey' who describes the route through Harthill village in the 1850s as being nothing more than a bridle track bounded at both the north and south ends by marshes.

"He used to tell how the way to Clowne was but a grass bridle track after leaving the village; how it passed through a rush-grown marsh in Nitticar Hollow; how the road, from where the school now stands (Whinney Lane) was lovely in summer time bordered by great overhanging trees, how Hard Lane in

summer time was a verdant tunnel of enclosing hawthorn and trees, leading by the foot of Harde Dam, and then on to the cross-roads across a marsh of reeds alive with water-fowl – the track for carts but roughly stoned. To-day's floods at Tommy Flockton's recall for us those days when Harthill in wet times was often isolated." ('Garbett, H. 1950. *The History of Harthill-w-Woodall and its hamlet Kiveton Park (the latter until AD 1868 when it becomes part of Wales parish)*, Ilfracombe, North Devon. 2nd impression 1978. Rotherham Libraries, Museum and Arts Department. P.54)'

Even if the OAN had not wanted to read as far as the 54th page of Garbett's book he clearly states the following within the first few pages of his book;

"As previously mentioned the road [Packman Lane] was always referred to as the 'Antient Way or Ye Streete' until the beginning of the 18th century; in fact it is frequently referred to as such during Tudor days. Local people then began to call it Packman Lane, because it was the nearest and best road to approach Harthill from a distance. Consequently it was used by

44

the Packmen when they became a feature of country social life in those days. It was, then, the only decent road approaching the village, for up to A.D. 1870 the roads to Kiveton, Killamarsh and Clowne were simply rough tracks with trees meeting overhead, and, beyond the village boundaries, simply bridle tracks.

It was a remarkable tribute this to Roman engineering, that their road was the best road in the district for a period of nearly 1,500 years." ('Garbett, H. 1950. *The History of Harthill-w-Woodall and its hamlet Kiveton Park (the latter until AD 1868 when it becomes part of Wales parish)*, Ilfracombe, North Devon. 2nd impression 1978. Rotherham Libraries, Museum and Arts Department. P.8).

I find it quite worrying that a supposed archaeological organisation such as the OAN did not read this account which is clearly visible within the first eight pages of Garbett's book. I also find it incredulous that the OAN cannot distinguish the difference between a modern road and an ancient road! On their evidence I am surprised that they have not suggested that the nearby M1 motorway is a Roman road because it *"includes a long linear stretch."*

There is no mention in these oral accounts that would suggest that there ever was a Roman road running through the centre of Harthill village itself, *'straight or otherwise,'* just a simple bridle track that ran through marsh land at the northern and southern ends of the village.

[c] Although Packman Lane is documented as being a Roman road its origins probably pre-date the Romans by several centuries and is probably of greater antiquity and possibly greater importance than originally thought!

CONCLUSION

As a layperson, I have identified in a short space of time several key areas in my report which clearly shows that the OAN's archaeological assessment of the area around Loscar Farm, for Npower Renewables is arrogant and flawed. The way the OAN has presented its evidence has been undertaken with little regard to producing a thoroughly researched and considered document of the proposed area around Loscar Farm.

The manner in which I was easily able to highlight key areas of importance that the OAN had overlooked or totally ignored despite their claims to the contrary in their report is, quite frankly an insult to the people of Harthill, Rotherham Borough Council and the people of Rotherham whom they arrogantly presume will accept their archaeological assessment as being thoroughly researched and true, when in fact, they can claim neither of these!

The OAN's report is amateurish, naïve and flippant. Their report for Npower, was so poorly researched, it is hard to actually believe or comprehend, because it is so easy to prove that they have not undertaken a thorough study of the area around Loscar Farm.

The fact that they did not even contact or consult the records at Derbyshire Record Office, nor contacted the Sites and

Monuments Officer there is beyond belief. And yet, they ask us to accept the findings of their report as believable and valid.

Based on my evidence here I suggest that the archaeological assessment produced by the OAN for National Wind Power Ltd., should be viewed with extreme caution and suspicion and subsequently disregarded by Rotherham Borough Council as it is nothing more than a whitewash written to commission for Npower Renewables, with the express view of finding as little archaeological evidence as possible, which is the one thing that they did do correctly!

HARTHILL ACTION GROUP.

Response to:

Loscar Farm Wind Turbines Proposed Development.

Report compiled by The Energy Workshop Ltd for John Wilks.

ACCESS FROM THE PUBLIC HIGHWAY AND THE REMOVAL OF THE ANCIENT HEDGEROWS.

By Paul Rowland.

SUMMARY

In a telephone conversation with Jim McNeil, Site and Monuments Officer of the South Yorkshire Sites and Monuments Records on Thursday 18th November 2004, with regard to Packman Lane, Harthill, Mr McNeil told me that he had travelled along Packman Lane in the past and said if the road is not Roman then it is certainly centuries old and the hedgerows will be of a similar age. This brings us to another issue of contention about the proposed development at Loscar Farm.

Mr McNeil also told me that there is now a *'Hedgerow Regulation'* in force which states that hedgerows cannot be removed without planning permission. And, it is up to Npower and their Archaeological Consultants to *prove* that the hedgerows are not of a significant age or importance.

Npower have *not* provided any information in their report that would *prove* that the hedgerows around Loscar farm are not of a significant age or importance!

INTRODUCTION

Npower Renewables state that the access to their proposed site along Packman Lane will be *"designed to accommodate the largest site construction vehicles and turning circle requirements. Site access will be via the existing field gate and access tracks that will be up-graded to allow for these requirements. A wider bell-mouth would be created to allow for access/turning and part of the existing hedgerow and grass verge (-36m either side) re-aligned to allow for adequate road safety, sight-lines and clearance."*

HARTHILL ACTION GROUP RESPONSE

Npower Renewables casually admit here that they intend to remove 72 metres of existing hedgerows alongside Packman Lane to allow access for their lorries and materials. This is a 237.6 foot long stretch of existing hedgerow which will be completely removed forever! This is a stretch of hedgerow that would span three quarters of the length of Sheffield Wednesday's football pitch! They also casually state that *"the existing field gate and access tracks... will be up-graded..."* This means road widening which they estimate will be increased in size from 3 metres to 6 metres – double the width of the current road! This they justify *"by increasing the width along the inner edge only"* will be necessary for them to *"accommodate the largest site construction vehicles,"* This they estimate to be 158 of the largest site construction lorries travelling daily to the site along Packman Lane to their proposed site for up to seven months!

There will also be a large 500-ton crane that will also have to be manoeuvred along Packman Lane to the proposed site to hoist their three giant structures into position. This will cause further irreparable damage to Packman Lane.

Npower have stated that they will not bring their lorries or turbines through Harthill or Thorpe Salvin to Loscar Farm. This means that they can only get to the site by approaching from the south along Bondhay Common, crossing Bondhay Dyke to the bottom of Mr Wilks' land and up Packman Lane to the site entrance. There is only one problem with that; and that is they will never be able to manoeuvre their lorries carrying the huge, rigid, wind turbine lengths, let alone a 500-ton crane around the double bend above Bondhay Dyke, without removing *'accidentally'* or otherwise the existing hedgerows and straightening the road which is thought to be the *'Whitwell Gap'* first mentioned in the Anglo-Saxon Chronicles in 942

A.D., and which was probably laid down a couple of millennia ago!

"The most outstanding environmental feature on the farm and throughout the whole area are the lines of mature and well established hedgerows. They host a variety of flora and fauna and act as route ways for invertebrates and birds linking green spaces across the intensively worked but ecologically barren arable fields." (Environmental Statement – Executive Summary. Chapter 3. 3.1.1, P.1.)

In their Environmental Statement – Executive Summary there are ten photographs listed, (chapter 3 – Wider Benefits Exec Summary, p.5) which shows where Npower plan to plant new hedgerows or build new fences on the site at Loscar Farm. All of these with the exception of photograph No.5 are within Mr Wilks' land at Loscar Farm. The photograph at No.5 has the caption, *"Typical gap in roadside boundary to be filled with post and rail fence."*

Npower's Environmental Statement – Executive Summary is simply an attempt by them to pacify the local population,

Rotherham Borough Council and all of the many other groups that are concerned about this proposed development at Loscar Farm. At first reading one may be misled into believing that Npower have every intention of making good any damage to the hedgerows by replanting and refencing. However, if one looks at the map of Loscar Farm produced by David Hetherington Environmental and Planning Services, one will see that all of the proposed replanting of hedgerows or re-fencing is all within Mr Wilks' land. The poor management of the fencing of the land at Loscar, as shown by the photographs in their report, is down to the land owner. The expense to repair or renew the existing fencing was probably another form of enticement used by Npower to site their wind turbines at Loscar Farm.

The stretch of hedgerow that separates the site from Packman Lane, is shown in their report (photograph No.5). This roadside boundary, is NOT to be replaced with '*new*' hedgerows, but with a post and rail fence! This is neither in-keeping with the existing lines of mature and well established hedgerows around the site area and neither is it acceptable!

Npower's characteristic *laissez-faire* attitude to the removal of a 237.6 foot long stretch of existing *"mature and well established hedgerow"* with no consideration to their age would be an act of wanton vandalism. These hedgerows are irreplaceable!

Npower states that; *"Inspection of the existing hedges shows that Hawthorn, Hazel, Blackthorn, Guilder Rose, Holly, Privet and Elder are all growing well where not punished too hard with the hedge-cutter."*

How old are the hedgerows around Loscar Farm and Packman Lane? One way to discover the age of a hedgerow is to count the number of different species growing in the hedge. It is universally accepted that the number of species growing within a hedgerow correlates to the age of the hedge in centuries!

It is interesting to note that Npower identified at least *seven* different species growing in the hedgerows around their proposed site at Loscar Farm and Packman Lane. This technique of hedgerow dating is known in archaeology as *'Hooper's Hypothesis.'*

HOOPER'S HYPOTHESIS

"M.D. Hooper noticed that it was difficult to account for the number of shrub species in a hedge simply through reference to its management, soil type or any other obvious factor. He suggested that the only correlation which did hold true for a wide sample of hedges was one which related the number of shrub species to the age of the hedge. The hypothesis is that the number of woody species in a 30 yard length of hedge equals the age of the hedge in centuries (Pollard, Hooper and Moore, 1974)." (Agate, Elizabeth. Hedging – A Practical Handbook, 1975, revised 2002, BTCV).

Some hedges are very ancient; many date from the Enclosures; some are less than a century old. Is it possible to look at an individual hedge and assign its age? Hedgerow dating is a subject of more than academic interest for two reasons:

a. Hedges of great antiquity have a historical value which makes them particularly worth protecting. Ancient hedges may be a genetic reservoir linking directly back to the ancient wildwood from which they were formed. It has also been suggested (Morgan Evans, in Watt and Buckley, 1994), that as *'man-made'* features they can be treated as artefacts and worthy of study by archaeologists. Historical value can only be recognised if the hedge can be dated by means of historical source material, field evidence or some inherent indicator of age.

b. Old hedges tend to have greater wildlife value due to their diversity of component species.

HISTORICAL RECORDS AND FIELD EVIDENCE

Written references to field boundaries in Britain can be traced back over a thousand years. County boundaries are among the earliest for which there is precise data, many of them dating from the middle of the 9th century. Anglo-Saxon land charters sometimes go into great topographical detail particularly where borders were disputed. Parish boundaries, which may date anywhere from the 7th or 8th to the 12th centuries, and later divisions within parishes, can be sought in old ecclesiastical records... *(ibid)*

Scrutiny of the 1:25,000 Ordnance Survey maps reveals a remarkable correlation between the lengths of hedged field boundaries, and multiples of a chain (22 yards, or about 20m). The most common length is 220 yards, or one furlong, i.e. one *'furrow long'.* Twelve and eight chain multiples are next most common, although other multiples may predominate in certain regions. All indications are that the chain has been the basic unit of hedgerow length for many centuries. In parts of north Norfolk, however, the most common field length is 410 yards. The area is rich in Roman roads and other remains, and this field length approximates two stadia, a Roman unit of measurement. The hedges themselves are probably not Roman, but the field boundaries may well be. *(ibid)*

The assumption is that species diversity will increase over time, as bird-ferried or windblown seeds take root in the shelter of the hedgerow. Regular trimming will help new species establish, by controlling existing species. The formula may also work because ancient hedges are more likely to be remnants of mixed woodland, or because hedges before about 1700 tended to be planted of mixed species.

However, the formula has been tested widely enough to give a reasonable degree of confidence that, used carefully, it can assist in dating hedges back to the Anglo-Saxon period. Current hedgerow regulations (Department of the Environment, 1997) use a count of woody species in a 30 metre length of hedgerow as one of the criteria for judging hedgerows as *'important'*. (Agate, Elizabeth. Hedging – A Practical Handbook, 1975, revised 2002, BTCV).

A survey of prehistoric and Roman iron agricultural implements in Britain (Morgan Evans, in Watt and Buckley, 1994) showed that heavy billhooks and lighter pruning tools were in use, possibly for cutting leaves for fodder, or for hedge trimming. Modern types of billhooks were in existence before the end of the Iron Age.

Along with literary evidence from Roman times of hedges in Italy and Flanders, this archaeological evidence indicates a strong possibility that there were hedges in Roman Britain.

Possible archaeological evidence goes back even farther, to the Bronze Age. At Shaugh Moor on Dartmoor, water-logged remains of hawthorn and rose were found, having been apparently cut and placed in a ditch. The hawthorn was 15 years old when cut. Split oak, possibly part of a fence and gateway were found, along with hoof prints which showed that the boundary was stockproof. The technology and techniques of coppicing go back as far as the Neolithic period, so hedges may have a very long history.

Have any of the Roman or Bronze Age hedges survived? Topographical analysis studies have shown extensive areas survive in England with pre-Roman boundaries. If continuity of use has allowed the survival of these boundaries, it could also imply that significant amounts of the hedgerow still survive.

Dead hedges, that is interwoven poles or brushy cuttings stuck in the ground, apparently were in use before Domesday as suggested by Anglo-Saxon manorial documents. Dead hedges are known to have been built to fence in deer from the start of the Tudor period (Pollard, Hooper and Moore, 1974). The dead hedge was the ancestor of the barbed wire fence, and as such immediately drops out of this history. However, it is owed a debt of gratitude as quite possibly allowing many early live hedges to spring up by providing a protected ungrazed strip for colonisation by hedge shrubs. This method of origin is the second of five recognised by Pollard, Hooper and Moore (1974) as possible for British hedges:

a. Hedges may have been formed around woodland clearings *(assarts)* made for agricultural purposes. These could either have been planted with shrubs taken from the woods, or may be relics of woodland plants managed to form hedges.

b. Hedges may have been formed by managing scrub growth which colonised field boundaries marked, and protected from grazing, by dead hedges.

c. They may have been planted as mixed hedges.

d. They may have been planted as single species hedges.

e. They may originate through a combination of factors.

Once in existence, hedges were exploited for all they offered including shelter, firewood and coppice timber, wild foods such as blackberries and hazelnuts, and small game especially birds. By medieval times these products were codified in law, with *'hedgebote'* being the right of commoners to use the hedgerow for fuel and branches to feed their stock in winter. *(Beddall, 1950). (ibid)*

The Enclosure movement, which in a sense started with the Celtic field clearances, really got underway in the 16th century, changing forever the open landscape of most of the country. Enclosures continued up to the mid 19th century. *(ibid)*

Parliamentary Enclosure Acts usually stipulated that newly enclosed lands be marked by boundary ditches, and then planted up with hedges on the bank created within. Work had to be finished within a year for the act to be binding, and suppliers of hedging shrubs did an increasingly brisk trade which verged on the frenzied by the middle of the 18th century.

These hedges were 'quickset', a word which indicates both the hedge itself and the act of planting such a hedge. LeSueur (1950) says that *'quick'* at first meant any living hedge, not necessarily of thorn as later understood. At this time the hedge was still a multipurpose item, coppice for fuel and fencing being as important as thorn for barring stock. He quotes Norden's advice (1607) that the best way to make a *'quick set'* is to mix the seeds of oak, thorn and ash together, wind them into a rough straw rope and bury the rope along the top of a bank.

As the rush to plant hedges continued, many people found employment gathering wild hawthorn seedlings from the woods. For many years, it was thought that these survived better when transplanted to a bank than would pampered *'nursery'* or *'garden quicks'*. However, by the 1790s it was realised that proper early care aided the survival and good growth of hedge shrubs. Soon the garden quick was being grown in vast numbers specifically for hedge plantations. Wild hawthorn seedlings may have been either of the two British species, *Crataegus monogyna*, known simply as hawthorn, or *Crataegus laevigata*, the *'woodland hawthorn'*. The garden quick however was exclusively *Crataegus monogyna*, and it is this species which has been the *'typical'* shrub of newly planted hedgerows ever since. A total of about 200,000 miles of hawthorn hedge was planted in the Parliamentary Enclosures of the 18th and 19th centuries (Mabey, 1996). (Agate, Elizabeth. Hedging – A Practical Handbook, 1975, revised 2002, BTCV).

CONCLUSION

Npower's arrogance and *laissez-faire* attitude to the proposed development at Loscar Farm is troubling. They have not attempted to prove beyond reasonable doubt that the hedgerows around Loscar Farm and Packman Lane are <u>NOT</u> of a significant age or importance as suggested by the South Yorkshire Sites and Monuments Records.

The hedgerows that Npower are proposing to remove without a second thought are of importance to Rotherham and to Harthill. Rotherham has some areas of outstanding natural beauty which it should endeavour to preserve at all costs for future generations, and not be blinded by the promise of an environmentally friendly *'quick fix'* that is nothing more than a wolf in sheep's clothing!

EVIDENCE OF ARCHAEOLOGY IN AND AROUND LOSCAR FARM, HARTHILL, SOUTH YORKSHIRE.

By Paul Rowland.

June 2007.

Since 1998 I have been studying the local history and archaeology of the village of Harthill with Woodall and the surrounding area in detail.

I was dismayed therefore to discover that the Reports submitted to Rotherham Metropolitan Borough Council first by Npower, and now by Cornish Light & Power were full of untruths and assumptions.

I was always told when I was studying archaeology that it was wise never to assume anything because it will always make an *"ASS"* out of *"U"* and *"ME."*

This however, is what Npower and CLP have done. They have assumed so many things that cannot be proven without a thorough examination and excavation of the proposed Loscar Farm site. Yet they expect, or hope that the RMBC will believe them and their archaeological consultants when they say that there is no archaeology to be found around the Loscar Farm site.

I should make it clear here, that unfortunately, I have been unable to obtain access to the Loscar Farm site to carry out my own archaeological survey, such as field walking or a metal detecting survey. As such I have had to rely on documentary evidence and aerial photography to prove my case against CLP's archaeological consultant's claims that there is no archaeology at Loscar Farm.

Both Npower, and Cornish Light & Power's archaeological reports have shown an ever decreasing area of archaeological interest. Their reports have shown that their area of interest has quickly shrunk from looking at the local area surrounding Loscar Farm, to only looking at archaeology within 1km of the

Loscar Farm site, to now only looking at the footprint of where the wind turbines will stand. The reason for this ever decreasing circle is blatantly obvious and clear for all to see. By choosing to ignore the archaeology all around Loscar Farm they are hoping that they can convince the RMBC that there is no need for 'ANY' archaeological investigation or excavations at Loscar Farm. Simply by choosing to ignore the archaeology on and around Loscar Farm won't make it go away, no matter how much CLP hope it will.

Loscar Farm cannot be viewed in isolation. The archaeology of this area is not limited to a current local farmer's boundaries. Remember, it was not until the 18th century that fields were finally enclosed. Before that most fields were open and ran one into the other, across land which is now enclosed and owned by several different farmers. As such, archaeology on one farmer's land may also relate to, and may be connected to the archaeology on a neighbouring farmer's land.

Using a piece of computer software called *Google Earth*, I have been able to study and measure archaeological features such as crop marks, enclosures and possible settlement sites in and around Loscar Farm.

Google Earth is a piece of free software that is available for anyone to use on the Internet. It uses NASA and European Space Agency satellite photographs of the world to visually record and map every corner of the globe. It was whilst looking at these free satellite photographs of the Loscar farm area that I discovered large scale archaeological features in and around Loscar Farm that clearly dispels CLP's archaeological consultants claims that there is no archaeology at Loscar Farm.

This evidence is available for all to see simply by going to the Internet and typing http://earth.google.com/download-earth.html into your web browser and downloading and installing the free software on your own computer. Once you have installed the software on your computer, simply enter the postcode S26 7XY for Loscar Farm into the *'Search'* window and Google Earth will automatically take you to this site on the globe.

By using the *'Historical Imagery'* button on Google Earth you will immediately be able to see clear evidence of archaeology in fields adjacent to Loscar Farm only a few feet away from Loscar farmland on the neighbouring land of Honeysykes

Farm. This is indisputable evidence that CLP cannot ignore any longer. This evidence is plain for all to see and the RMBC would be wise to consider this evidence very carefully. Its close proximity to Loscar Farm probably suggests that the

archaeology on the neighbouring farm of Honeysykes farmland is not isolated only to Honeysykes Farm but probably spreads a few metres west across Packman Lane onto Loscar farmland also.

Figure 1: View looking north showing the farms of Loscar Farm, (top left) and, its immediate neighbour Honeysykes Farm at Harthill. These two farms are separated only by Packman Lane, a narrow lane 9ft wide that is believed to have once been a Roman road. This photograph shows indisputable evidence of the extensive and complex archaeology around Loscar Farm. Also note the diagonal lines on Loscar farmland running across the plough lines at the top left of the photo. Are these archaeological or geological features?

It is impossible from aerial photographs alone to precisely date the possible archaeology shown below Honeysykes Farm. However, it is probable that this site could possibly date from the iron age (800-750 B.C). D.N. Riley stated in his book, *Early Landscape from the air – Studies of Crop Marks in South Yorkshire & North Nottinghamshire. 1980., p.46*) *"It is interesting to note that in East Yorkshire, where the crop marks have received close study by the Royal Commission on Historical Monuments, the larger oval or circular enclosures were almost always of iron age origin."* A circular feature can be seen here inside a much larger oval enclosure. (see diagram below).

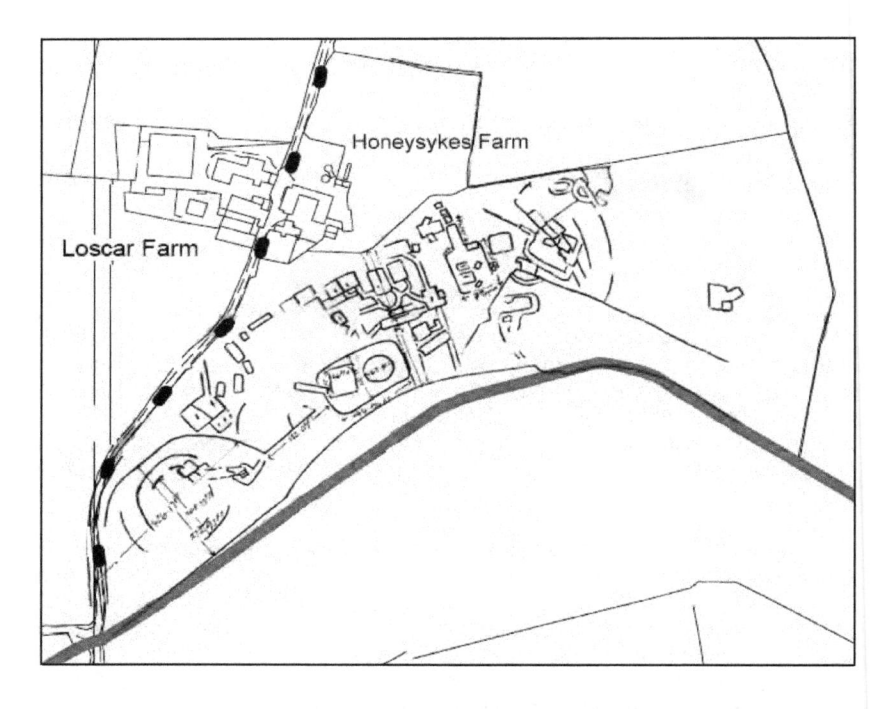

Figure 2: Above is an outline map of some of the more distinguishable features in the south field of Honeysykes Farm, Harthill with measurements. The oval enclosure and the possible circular feature can be seen in more detail below.

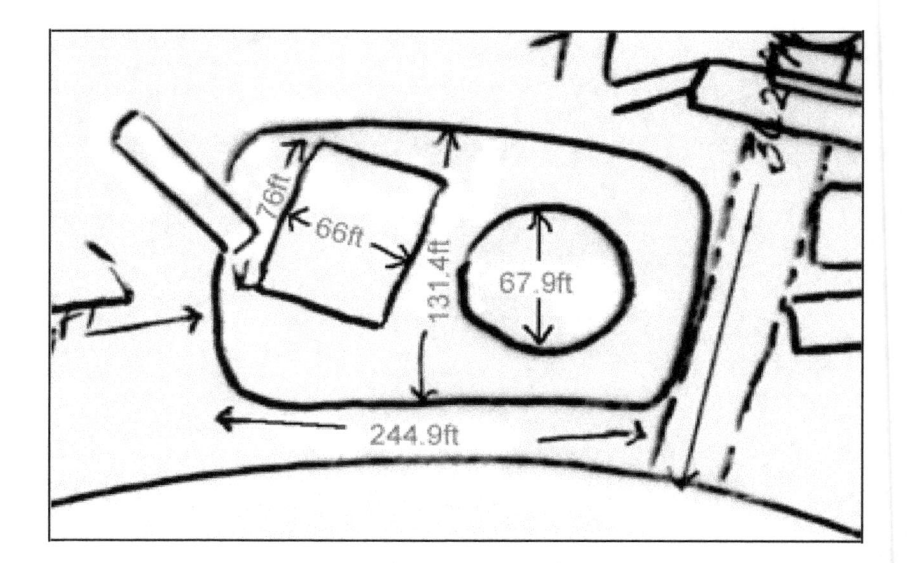

Figure 3. Approximate measurements using Google Earth of the *possible* oval enclosures surrounding a square and *possible* circular enclosures. Could the circular enclosure be an iron age round house? Are these features archaeological or geological?

Figure 4: View of crop marks in the south field of Honeysykes Farm looking west towards Loscar Farm, Harthill. The oval enclosure feature can be clearly seen at the bottom (left) of the field. Notice also, the large circular enclosure feature (top left) at the southernmost tip of this field adjoining Packman Lane.

Figure 5: View of south field, looking south west across Loscar farmland. Notice how Packman lane curves around the large circular roadside enclosure feature at the tip of this field. This could suggest that Packman lane, came into existence at the same time as, or shortly after the large circular roadside enclosure feature was built possibly in the iron age.

If Packman lane had come into existence long after the

enclosure had fallen into disuse it would have been probable

74

that the trackway, and then the road would have taken a direct line through the enclosure rather than sweeping around it to preserve its boundary.

Figure 6: Overhead view of the oval enclosure feature and crops marks in the south field at Honeysykes Farm, Harthill. Loscar Farm can be seen in the bottom right hand corner of this photograph across the narrow Packman Lane, opposite Honeysykes Farm.

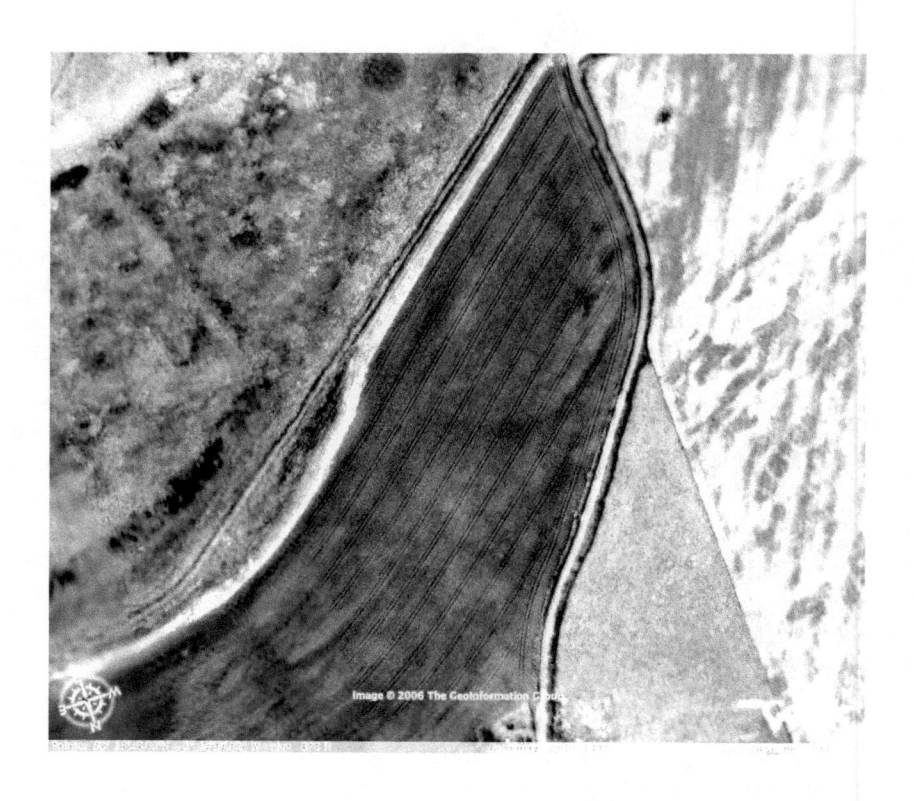

Figure 7: Overhead view of the oval enclosure feature and the large roadside enclosure feature in the south field at Honeysykes Farm, Harthill. It is possible that part of this large circular enclosure feature may continue further south onto the waste land of Bondhay Golf Course.

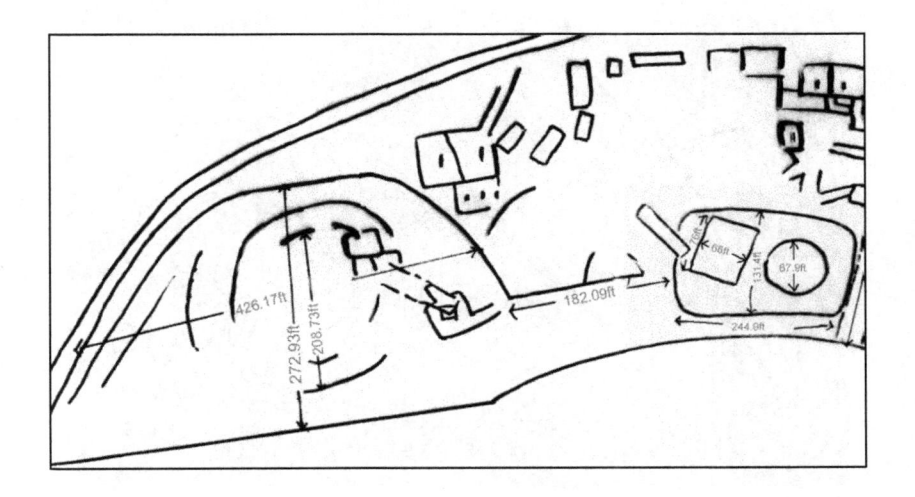

Figure 8: Above is an outline map looking west showing approximate measurements (taken using Google Earth) of the possible large circular roadside enclosure features on Honeysykes Farm's south field, situated next to Packman Lane, Harthill.

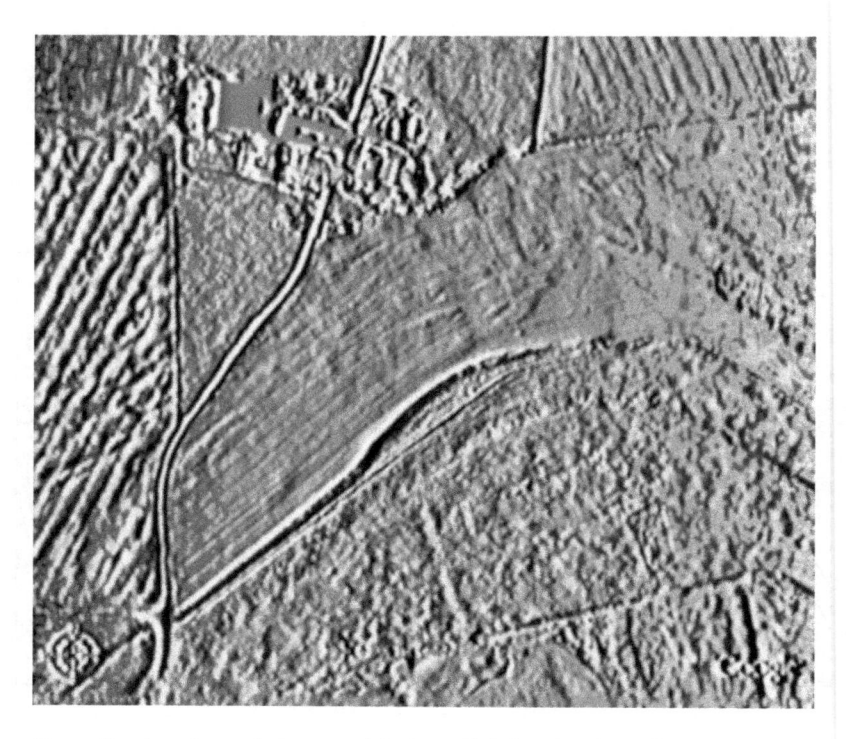

Figure 8a: An enhanced photograph in bas relief showing the archaeology on the south field at Honeysykes Farm.

Figure 9. View looking north east at the crop marks on Honeysykes Farm. Note the close proximity of these features to Loscar Farm. Also note the diagonal marks running across the plough lines on the field below Loscar Farm. Are these archaeological or geological features?

Figure 10: Another view showing the crop marks at Honeysykes Farm and more of the diagonal crop marks below Loscar Farm.

The nearby site of Scratta Wood, according to (Challis and Harding 1975:94) in D.N. Riley's book, *Early Landscape from the air – Studies of Crop Marks in South Yorkshire & North Nottinghamshire. 1980., p.70*) is *"an important iron age settlement."* Scratta Wood is recorded in the South Yorkshire Archaeology Service's records. It is situated only a short distance west of Honeysykes Farm, but it is not as extensive or as complex as the site I have discovered at Honeysykes Farm, Harthill.

Using Google Earth I have discovered large areas of archaeology on and around Loscar Farm that proves without doubt that there is in fact quite a sizeable area of archaeology in the Loscar Farm, Harthill and Thorpe Salvin area.

This archaeology is probably all interconnected and its possible destruction at the hands of CLP must be taken into account when considering the proposed wind farm development at Loscar Farm. Would the RMBC want to sanction the destruction of a site of possible archaeological importance without a proper and thorough examination and excavation of the area, especially when the archaeological evidence is plain for the whole world to see?

On a visit to the South Yorkshire Archaeology Service last year to check my discovery at Honeysykes Farm, I was amazed to discover that the SYAS has no record of these enclosures at Honeysykes Farm, and hardly any record of archaeology at all in the Harthill area. When I asked Mr Jim McNeil of the South Yorkshire Archaeology Service why that was, he stated that; *"people imagine the SYAS to have a record of every item and every place of archaeological interest in the South Yorkshire area, but this is not the case. We only know about these places if people bring them to our attention."* He said.

Mr Karl Noble of Rotherham Museum also told me that Harthill was probably the least well documented area of the whole of the Rotherham Metropolitan Borough, and the museum only gets to know about finds etc., if they are reported to the museum. *"It is not because there is no archaeology in the Harthill and Loscar Farm area, it is simply because people choose not to disclose their finds, and as such it has never been brought to the attention of Rotherham Museum nor the SYAS."* That is why the SYAS and Rotherham Museum has so little information about the area surrounding Harthill and the Loscar Farm Area.

The archaeology I have discovered at Honeysykes Farm is completely unknown and unrecorded and I am bringing it to the attention of the public for the first time in this document in the hope that thorough investigations and excavations of the archaeology in this area will be deemed to be a necessary requirement before it is allowed to be destroyed by the development of a windfarm at Loscar Farm.

If you look at Google Earth, or the photographs and maps contained within this report, you will notice evidence of settlement and farming stretching between Harthill and Thorpe Salvin across Loscar Farm and beyond. It would appear from these photographs that Loscar Farm and the area between Harthill and Thorpe Salvin was probably more densely populated than it is today. I have not attempted to record all of the evidence around Loscar Farm of the enclosures or field systems that can be clearly seen using Google Earth. Instead I have concentrated only on areas in close proximity to Loscar Farm as the evidence is too numerous to record in the time available to me to submit this report to the RMBC Planning Department.

There is evidence of early *Brickwork Field Systems* north, south, east and west of Loscar Farm and also across Honeysykes Farm and Loscar Farm. *Brickwork Field Systems* were first identified by D.N. Riley in 1973 and were found to be most common in north Nottinghamshire and Yorkshire south of the River Don. Harthill is the southernmost point of South Yorkshire and it's southern boundary joins the north Derbyshire and north Nottinghamshire boundaries.

Riley coined the phrase *Brickwork Field System* because the layout of the fields he discovered resembled *"the pattern formed by the joints in a brick wall... formed by long parallel ditches, between which are strips of land generally from 50 to 100 m wide. Cross boundary ditches cut the strips into fields, the greater number of which are from 0.5 to 2.8 ha in area. Some of the long boundaries are formed by two parallel ditches, which might have had a bank between them. Enclosures are joined to the field boundaries in places. This was a planned system of land division, perhaps partly controlled by the physical geography, because the long boundaries tend to run at right angles to the general direction of the courses of the rivers, but it was not standardised, and there are differences in the field plans from north to south of the region."* (Riley D.N. 1980. Early Landscape from the air – Studies of Crop Marks in South Yorkshire & North Nottinghamshire. p.11).

"The field plans shown by crop marks may be divided into three varieties, the brickwork plan, found in many places, and the nuclear and irregular plans, which are less frequent." (Riley D.N. ibid. p.11).

Nuclear Plan Fields

"An enclosure forms the centre of each block of nuclear plan fields, and the name has been chosen because of these central nuclei. They have only been found so far [in 1980] in or near the parish of Rossington, South Yorkshire. [Loscar Farm is approximately 21.4 km away from Rossington as the crow flies]. These plans include strips, and have some relationship with the brickwork pattern, but the strips are in small blocks,

fitted together at right angles in a patchwork pattern." (Riley D.N. ibid. p.11).

With field systems described as the nuclear plan, it is thought that each nucleus was probably a farmstead, surrounded by the fields that went with it.

"The occurrence of small blocks of strips within nuclear field plans, and the similarity of the field dimensions in the brickwork and nuclear plans, makes it probable that the two plans were related." (Riley D.N. ibid. p.19).

Figure 11: Evidence of Nuclear Plan Fields 21.4 km south of Rossington which was believed to be the only place these types of fields existed. These fields lie only 970.9 metres west of Loscar farmland. The indication of several nuclei seen in this photograph would suggest that there is the possibility of a unified settlement site, rather than a solitary farmstead.

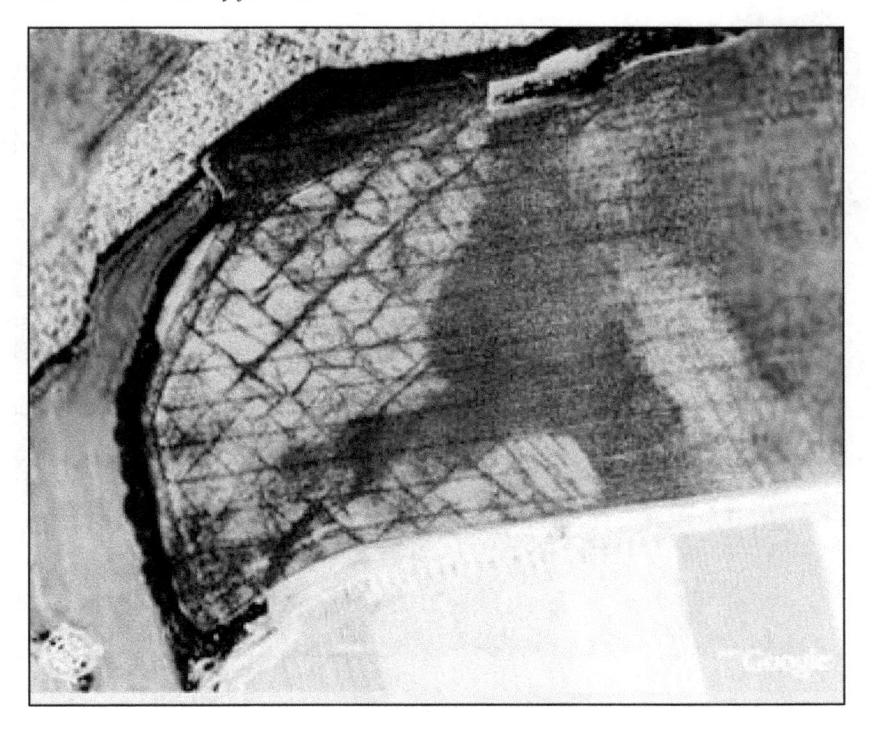

Figure 11a: A clearer black and white photograph of the Nuclear Plan field system shown in Fig. 11. Is this archaeological or geological?

Figure 11b. This photograph shows evidence of more Nuclear and Brickwork Plan Field Systems next to the field containing the distinct Nuclear Plan Field System shown in Figure 11.

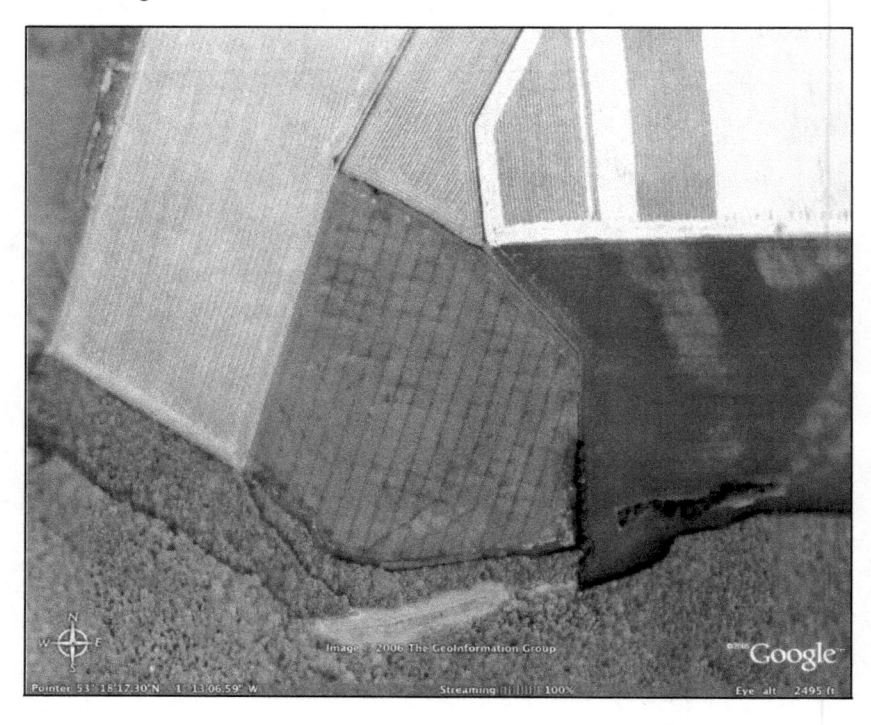

Figure 11c: *A clearer black and white photograph of the field system shown in Fig. 11b.*

Figure 12: Continuation of the Nuclear Plan Field Systems and enclosures as shown in Fig. 2., showing the large expanse of land that these field systems and enclosures covered. More evidence of the large extent of these field systems can be seen immediately east of Whitwell Wood using Google Earth.

Figure 13: A closer view of more Nuclear Plan Field Systems as shown in Fig. 2., and Fig. 3., showing how the Nuclear Plan Field System and the Brickwork Plan Field Systems were, as Riley suggested, probably related.

Irregular Plan Fields

"The irregular plan fields, which approximate to rectangular shape, cover small areas, generally on low ground, or near rivers. They are somewhat different from the other types of

91

field plans. Lanes are often seen between these fields." (Riley D.N. ibid. p.11).

Brickwork Plan Fields

"The brickwork plan fields were in use in the later Roman period, though their period of origin is uncertain. The nuclear plan fields may be earlier, and it is suggested that they were of pre-Roman origin. No information on date is known about the irregular plan in this region." (Riley D.N. ibid. p.11).

Each of these three field systems can be seen in and around the Loscar farm, Harthill and Thorpe Salvin area.

Figure 14: Evidence of the Brickwork Plan Field System running north east from Honeysykes Farm towards Thorpe Salvin. The map coordinates can be seen at the bottom of the photograph for anyone to view these crop marks for themselves on Google Earth.

Figure 15: This bas relief photograph of the field in Figure 14. clearly shows evidence of the Brickwork Plan Field System east of Honeysykes Farm.

Figure 15a: More Brickwork Plan Field Systems north of Honeysykes Farm, Harthill.

Figure 16: Evidence of the extent of the early Brickwork Plan Field System can be clearly seen stretching north east from Honeysykes Farm, across to the neighbouring village of Thorpe Salvin. At Honeysykes there is Brickwork Plan field systems but as it gets nearer to Thorpe Salvin the field system changes to Irregular Plan field systems and Nuclear Plan field systems the closer it gets to the village of Thorpe Salvin. Perhaps this proves that Riley's theory that these three types of field systems were all related is correct.

Riley explained the reason why these three types of field plans occur predominately in this area. *"The first paragraph of the account of Nottinghamshire in Gibson's edition of Camden's*

Britannia includes the statement 'The west part is entirely took up with the forest of Shirwood, which is very large. This part, because it is sandy, the inhabitants call the Sand; the other, because it is clayish, they call the Clay; and thus have they divided their county into these two parts.' The clay referred to is the heavy soil on the Keuper Marl, and the sand is the deposit described in this account as the Bunter Sandstone, two formations which outcrop in long bands of country between Nottingham and Doncaster, covering much of Nottinghamshire, and extending well into South Yorkshire. Soils on the Bunter deposits often develop crop marks on a very large scale..." (Riley D.N. ibid. p.1).

Riley discovered that *"the soils with crop marks are restricted to land above a few geological formations, the Bunter Pebble Beds, the narrow adjacent outcrop of the Lower Mottled Sandstone, and various associated gravels and sandy boulder clays, which for convenience are here referred to collectively as the Bunter Sandstone area. These permeable deposits are covered by soils prone to dessication in the time of drought, so that the right conditions exist for the development of crop marks. They also produce soft subsoil's, into which it is very easy to dig, with the result that early man covered the land with ditches in the course of farming work, and thus made the disturbances which affect crops at the present day. Some of the sandy soils have limitations as farm land, but at some period they were evidently exploited on a large scale by early man."* (Riley D.N. ibid. p.2).

These formations underlie a belt of country up to nine miles (fourteen kilometres) wide, which runs south from the River Don through Yorkshire and Nottinghamshire (Map 1). The crop marks occur largely on the northern and central parts of this territory from Doncaster to Mansfield. It is interesting to note that near Mansfield the little River Meden formed the northern boundary of the land under the forest law of the mediaeval Sherwood Forest (Boulton 1965:36), an area in which there is apparently much less to be recorded from the air." (Riley D.N. ibid. p.2).

Figure 17: An aerial view of the south field at Loscar Farm. Please note the diagonal marks running across the plough lines in the field. Upon close examination these diagonal marks appear to be connected to one another at right angles in strips and run parallel to the Brickwork Plan Field Systems that can be clearly seen in the fields at Honeysykes Farm. Are these archaeological or geological features

Figure 18: Another view of the south field at Loscar Farm showing that the diagonal lines running across the Loscar farmland also extends into the fields across the road on the same parallel line to the Brickwork Plan Field Systems on Honeysykes Farm. It was in this field that the majority of finds were discovered by Npower's archaeological consultants Oxford Archaeology North. It is also across this field that CLP plans to bring their heaviest lorries to deliver their heavy machinery and their wind turbines to the Loscar Farm site.

Figure 18a: Evidence of Brickwork Plan field system in the field across the road from, and below Loscar Farm's south field.

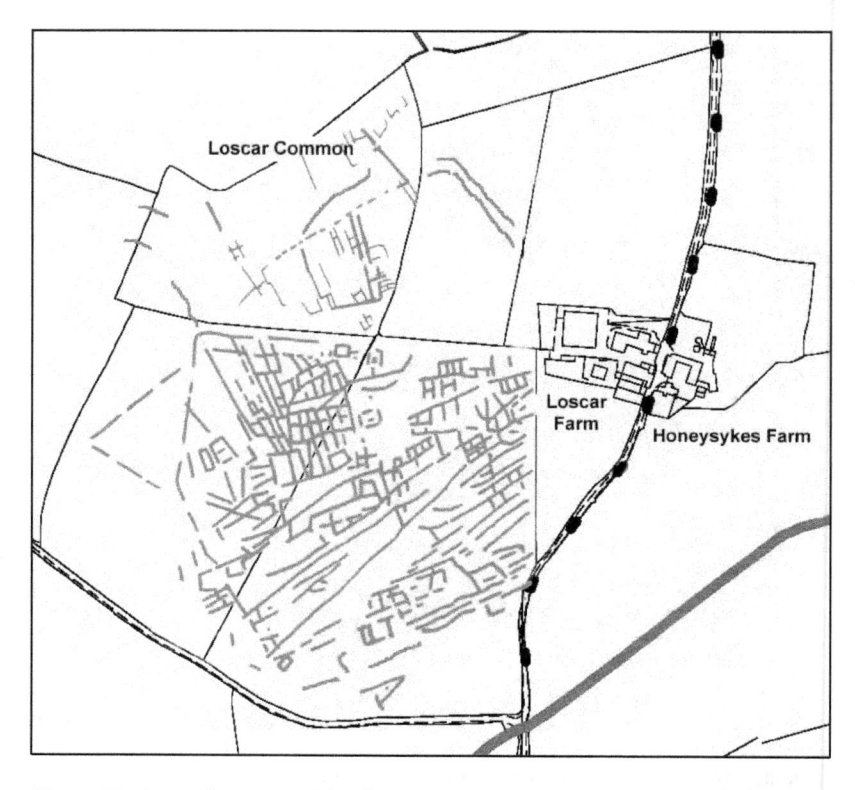

Figure 19: An outline map of the diagonal lines and interconnected strips that can be seen on the south field of Loscar Farm. These numerous *possible* enclosures are probably the reason why that the majority of finds were discovered here by OAN. The south facing slopes of Loscar Farm and Honeysykes Farm, like sites elsewhere would have almost certainly been the main habitation area of early man as they would benefit from the warmth of the sun.

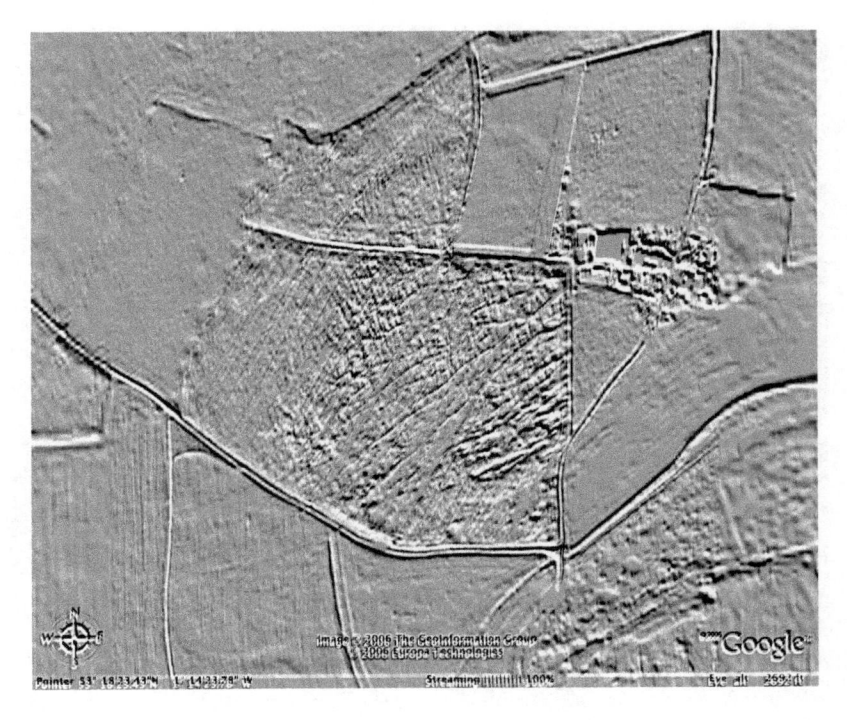

Figure 20: This bas relief photograph of the south field of Loscar Farm clearly shows the diagonal strips and the irregular plan field system that run parallel to the early field system that stretches from Honeysykes Farm to Thorpe Salvin.

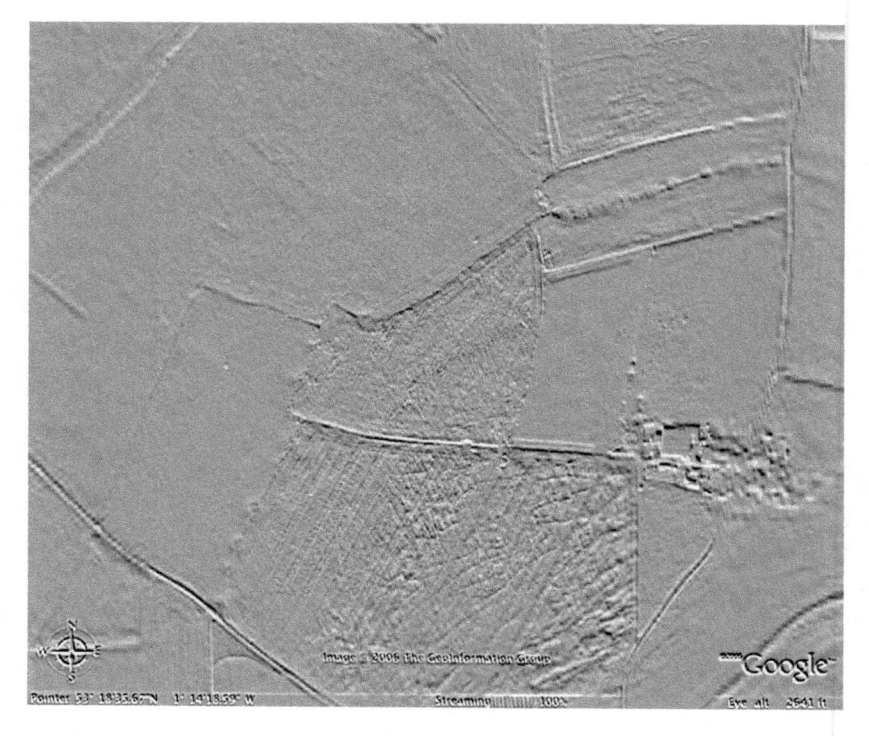

Figure 20a: This bas relief photograph of the south field at Loscar Farm shows evidence of more enclosures in the field directly above it. Evidence of an Irregular Plan field system can also be seen in this field.

"The remains revealed by crop marks differ considerably in various parts of England. In this region the principal things seen are the boundaries of extensive systems of fields and of many enclosures, single or in clusters. The fields are in many places arranged in parallel strips and the enclosures are

often joined to the field boundaries, with which they were no doubt contemporary. <u>This was a planned system of land use, covering large tracts of country.</u> There are also occasional patches of fields of less regular plan, but they cover much smaller areas. Few remains occur of some kinds of monuments frequent in other parts of England where there are many crop marks, for example the circles which indicate the ditches of ploughed out round barrows or other ritual sites. To the aerial observer, the restricted range of types of crop marks suggests that the early history of the Bunter Sandstone region was simpler than that of other parts of the country." (Riley D.N. ibid. p.2).

"Although the early fields are so extensive," Riley explained, "there was initially no information about their date, except that at one point they are crossed by a Roman road." (Riley D.N. ibid. p.2).

At Harthill, it is widely believed that Packman Lane was a Roman road. It would be inconceivable to believe, looking at the photographs in this report that the Romans did not press

Packman Lane into use during their long occupation of Britain. However, its origins probably pre-date the Romans judging from the way Packman Lane sweeps around the large roadside enclosure at Honeysykes Farm.

Although sporadic Roman artefacts have been found along Packman Lane, no real evidence of the Roman road has ever been found. With the exception of the 4 inch dressed cobbles that I discovered at the Packman Lane crossroads a few years ago. However, without a proper excavation of that site it seems likely that developers will refuse to accept Packman lane was ever a Roman road despite the long oral and documentary evidence that suggests otherwise.

Thanks to Google Earth, there is clear evidence to suggest that the Roman road that Derbyshire SMR recorded running north from Markland Grips on an alignment with Packman lane, but which they unfortunately lost in the fields south of Harthill may have been rediscovered.

If one looks at the photograph below of the south field at

Honeysykes Farm, a long dark straight feature runs from the bottom of the field to the top until it stops at the Honeysykes farmhouse. It can be seen running in a north to south direction and touches the right-hand edge of the oval enclosure. This feature is approximately 315ft in length and it is 60ft wide.

Figure 21: Is the long dark straight feature running north to south through the field at Honeysykes Farm, evidence of the existence of the Roman road at Harthill?

When I first looked at this feature (Fig. 21) I thought it was probably evidence of hedgerow removal. However I looked at photographs from the National Monuments Records of this field and it did prove that there was once a hedgerow running in a north to south direction across this field. However, upon closer inspection and by overlaying the two photographs I discovered that the location of the hedgerow was more than 60 feet away to the right of this feature, on the eastern side of the field. This area requires more archaeological investigation to determine its importance nationally.

Figure 21a: Photograph from the National Monuments Records showing the south field of Honeysykes and Loscar Farms. The position of the former hedgerow can be clearly seen in this 1971 photograph of Honeysykes farrmland. The oval enclosure has been overlaid to show that the hedgerow was situated more than 60ft away to the right of the dark feature that can be seen running through this field. Is this dark feature the route of the Roman road?

Riley believed that *"it may in due course be possible to*

study the general patterns of early land divisions over a wide area, including the Bunter Sandstone country, which will then perhaps be linked with important landscapes further afield, such as the Yorkshire Wolds, the Roman Fenland or the celtic fields of Wessex." (Riley D.N. ibid. p4).

"In addition to the geology it is necessary to consider the local changes at the points where crop marks appear, that is the material filling the ancient ditches and pits, now buried beneath the surface... In the 1976 excavations the plough soil at Flint Hill, Elkesley and Green Mile Lane, Babworth varied from 25 to 35 cm in depth, below which the ditch fillings were brown sandy soil, not easy to distinguish from the undisturbed orange to yellow sand or sandy gravel. From a visual inspection of the sections it seemed remarkable that such slight changes in the ground should have produced growth differences in crops. At some other excavated sites, elsewhere in England, ditch fillings have proved to be much more clearly differentiated from their

surroundings. In the Upper Thames valley, for example, the fillings of ring ditches were often found to be composed of fine brown earth, very different from the adjacent gravel (Leeds 1936:11), and it is much easier to understand the development of crop marks on such sites. The filling of disturbances in the ground varies greatly according to local circumstances at most archaeological sites, but the geology has had a general effect on ditch fillings everywhere." (Riley D.N. ibid. p.7). The reported shallow depth of soil on certain parts of Loscar farmland may produce similar results.

"It will be seen that the strips are narrower in the northern part [of the Bunter Sandstone area] with many examples of only 50 m and that to the south, unusually wide strips occur occasionally... The majority are between 70 and 100 m wide. There is a suspicion that there were modules of about 50 m to 90 m and 200 m... " (Riley D.N. ibid. p.14). There are some strips around Loscar and Honeysykes Farms that are approximately 45 m wide.

"The evidence, cited subsequently, for use of the brickwork plan in the Roman period raises the possibility of planning by a formal method. There are no signs of centuriation, but consideration must be given to land allocation in strips by the methods termed in lacineis or per strigas by classical writers (Bradford 1957:212; Dilke 1971:95). It could be suggested that the widths of 50, 90 and 200 m, to which the brickwork plan strips approximate, resembled Roman units of 11/2, 3 and 6 actus (equivalent to 53, 106, and 213 m in modern units), but the strips vary so much that this idea is difficult to support." (Riley D.N. ibid. p.16). It is interesting to note that the early field systems on and around Loscar Farm all follow the same NE/SW alignment, which does suggest that the extensive field systems around Loscar Farm were part of a planned layout.

"The fields are often in large blocks, which may cover as much as 200ha, and it may be asked whether these blocks are part of much greater areas of fields, or whether they were units surrounded by land which was not divided by field boundaries." (Riley D.N. ibid. p.16). The evidence at

Harthill does suggest that the archaeology and the field systems on Honeysykes Farm and Loscar Farm, and in the surrounding countryside was all connected. As such this archaeology must be viewed collectively and examined in more detail to gain better understanding of the early history of this part of the Rotherham Metropolitan Borough.

Purpose Of The Fields

Information based on air photographs alone cannot determine the purpose for which the fields were intended and excavation is needed to provide evidence, assuming that there are places where the debris of farming or traces of the former environment survive. A few facts can, however, be assembled which have a bearing on the subject.

The land near the rivers would have been suitable for meadows to be grazed by stock, but higher up the sandy soil on the ridges between the rivers would have been too dry in summer to be good for grassland. It would also have been liable to become infested with bracken. These light soils would have been ploughed easily with primitive equipment, but their acid nature would only have suited oats or rye. *(Russell 1973:661),* and crops of other cereals would have been poor, in the absence of lime which is applied by farmers at the present day.

The fields are typically from 1 to 2 ha (2 1/2 to 5 acres) in size, which is about ten times as big as the 0.1 and 0.6 ha (1/4 to 1 1/2 acres) *'Celtic'* fields of Wessex (Bowen 1961:20). The latter were ploughed, and the big Bunter Sandstone fields if cultivated with similar ploughs, might have been sub-divided into smaller plots. This is a question about which no useful evidence has yet been found locally. In the absence of crop marks showing sub-divisions, the only way in which they would be traced would be to find intact remains of the early fields in places which had escaped later ploughing. In Nottinghamshire such places possibly exist in the forests, but the slight remains of the fields would be extremely difficult to see among the trees and bracken.

Could the early Brickwork Field Systems that I have highlighted here around Loscar and Honeysykes Farms, provide that evidence?

"Before the subject is left, it may be worth mentioning an interesting parallel in a rather distant part of England: the 'Celtic' fields at Aldsworth and Eastleach in Gloucestershire (R.C.H.M. 1976:2) These fields are planned in a framework of parallel strips, bounded by the ruins of stone walls. At one place strips from 53 to 57 m wide – very similar to the narrower Bunter Sandstone brickwork pattern strips – are divided into plots of about 0.15 to 0.2 ha (1/3 to 1/2 acre) by cross lynchets 0.5 to 1 m high. The plan of the resulting small fields might be described as a 'ladder' pattern, with frequent cross boundaries, and it is not impossible that this was the original appearance of some South Yorkshire and Nottinghamshire fields." (Riley D.N. ibid. p.26). There is evidence of what may be a small Ladder Pattern field system on Loscar Farm itself.

Enclosures

"Among the fields are often seen enclosures, that is, areas surrounded by a ditch and apparently intended as living areas or for special purposes." (Riley D.N. ibid. p.27).

"The crop marks of enclosures are often broader and darker in colour than those of the fields, from which it may be surmised that their ditches were often wider and deeper than those dug at field boundaries, though in some cases the darker crop mark might have been caused by other factors, such as occupation material in the ditch filling. They normally have rounded corners, and may not be quite in line with the field boundaries they adjoin, as if they had been planned separately, but this is not always the case, and reference is made below to the difficulty in deciding which crop mark shapes should be called enclosures.

The term enclosure may itself be a little ambiguous, because it could also be used to describe a field...[or] a piece of ground used for pasturage or tillage. The Enclosure Acts for example, were concerned with the division of the medieval open fields into the fields of the present day, enclosed by fences. In archaeological literature, however, the word enclosure has come to mean not a field but a ditched or embanked area used for some special purpose and it is in that sense that it is used here." (Riley D.N. ibid. p.27).

"Crop mark plans show only a part, perhaps a small part, of the total disturbance of the soil by early man, which can only be revealed fully by excavation." (Riley D.N. ibid. p. 29).

The RMBC cannot allow the destruction of the Loscar Farm site to proceed without first demanding a thorough investigation and excavation of the site and the area surrounding Loscar Farm.

"By analogy with excavated sites in many other parts of England, the enclosures were no doubt used as dwelling sites, or for various farming purposes. There is evidence to confirm their use as dwelling sites at a few places in the region, where traces of round houses were seen within

enclosures...or where Romano-British pottery was found in some quantity." (Riley D.N. ibid. p.34).

There is clear evidence within this report to suggest that the unrecorded sites of a *possible* iron age round house, numerous enclosures and early field systems exists only a few metres away from Loscar Farm. Does the RMBC want to be held responsible for allowing the destruction of extensive and unrecorded archaeology in this area without a proper and thorough archaeological excavation in and around Loscar Farm?

When Riley studied the Bunter Sandstone soils and early agriculture, he suggested that *"buried ancient soils have still to be located and studied."* (Riley D.N. ibid. p.70). We have a unique opportunity to rediscover the past amongst the archaeology in these very early field systems around Loscar and Honeysykes Farms that I have pointed out in this report.

Riley also made this point; *"The soils elsewhere in South Yorkshire and north Nottinghamshire are very different. To the east the badly drained clay soils of the Keuper Marl outcrop cannot have been easy to work by early man, and are rated from Class 2 to Class 4 at the present day by the Soil Survey. To the west, the Magnesian Limestone belt has friable and well drained loams, rated in Classes 1 and 2, on which, for example, an important iron age settlement at Scratta Wood, near Worksop (Challis and Harding 1975:94)...are known. This good land was probably well exploited in early times, though it does not produce crop marks like the Bunter Sandstone and early fields therefore cannot be traced."* (Riley D.N. ibid. p.70).

Scratta Wood is a short distance away to the west of Honeysykes Farm. This settlement is recorded in the South Yorkshire Archaeological Services records, but it is not as extensive or as complex as the site I have discovered at Honeysykes Farm, and which has not yet been recorded by the SYAS.

Riley describes the maps of these early field systems that he produced in his book, *Early Landscapes* as *"its most valuable contents and should make a lasting contribution to local archaeology.*" (Riley D.N. ibid. p.1). I also hope that the information presented here will now disprove many of the untruths that the developers of the proposed windfarm at Loscar Farm have continually told. It is unfortunate, but the evidence contained in this report proves that the developer's archaeological consultants are either inept or have been found to be economic with the truth!

I would ask the RMBC to consider the following archaeological evidence to be taken into account against CLP's archaeological consultant's findings.

Below is further evidence of the archaeology surrounding Loscar farm.

The Burr Well

Harthill's Burr Well, once supplied fresh water to the village of Harthill and more famously to The Duke of Leeds' residence at Kiveton Hall. The name of this well has always intrigued me because of its reference to a *Burh* even though it is spelt differently to the word *Burh* which means *'a fortified settlement.'* On every map I have looked at over the years there is no evidence of any Burh near the site of the Burr Well.

However, in 2006, using Google Earth I was able to look closely at the Burr Well and study the ancient scars and archaeological features that I could see in the Harthill landscape.

From the entrance of the now derelict Burr Well I was able to measure the width of the water flow that gushed from the mouth of the well. The watercourse can be clearly seen and it probably once ran through woodland before it was cleared for farming.

Burr Well, Harthill

Common Road

View Looking East

Figure 22: View looking east across the sloping fields towards the Burr Well, from Serlby Lane, Harthill.

Figure 22a: The photograph above shows Harthill's Burr Well as it appears today. It appears as a mound in the field (middle left) with a brickwork entrance blocked by locked iron gates. The well was damaged in recent times by the farmer whilst ploughing the field and no longer produces water. The Well is now dry. The water that once flowed from the Burr Well rose from underground similar to the water that rises from the limestone gorge at Malham Cove in the Yorkshire Dales.

Evidence of this underground water source can still be seen today a short distant north from the Burr Well on the former football field near Kiveton Park Station. The centre of the field is continually wet and boggy and at the bottom of the field water can be seen bubbling up from below the surface.

During the sale of the Duke of Leeds estate in the 1920s, the field at Kiveton Park Station states that the field (which is now the football field) had a *'limitless'* supply of fresh water from the underground well at the bottom corner of the field, adjacent to Packman Lane. This water supply was later capped and a small water pump house was erected over the well.

From the aerial photographs it is clear to see the course that the water from the Burr Well used to take through a field that was once known as Hawk Wood. It meanders for a short way before it runs into the side of the field and continues north into the Thurgosyke stream.

Figure 22: The width of the watercourse that carried the water from the Burr Well was twenty feet wide. This was a considerable volume of water and would have been a major reason for placing a Burh or settlement close to it. With a large supply of fresh water gushing close by, it would make great sense to build a settlement here. But where exactly?

Aerial Photographic Evidence

Turning to Google Earth again, I noticed a number of scars and a couple of bends in the roads that obviously went around some existing feature. However, when one looks at the 1720 map of Harthill's South and Middle Fields, there is no sign or evidence on that map of any discernible feature whatsoever. The roads to Harthill running South to North were Carr Lane (the current main road running past Carr Farm which joined Winney Hill and continued into Union Street through to Kiveton. And, Packman Lane, to the East.

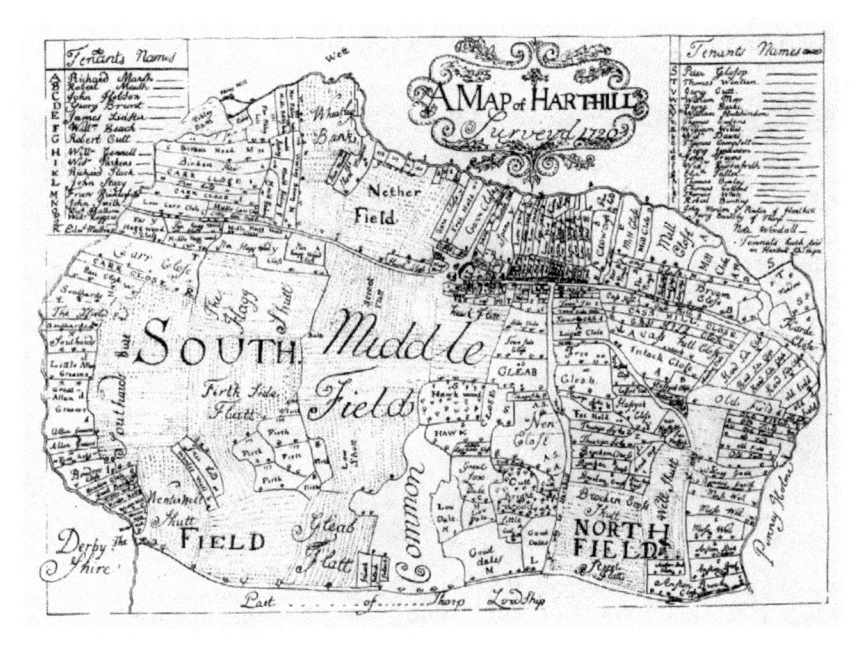

Figure 23: The 1720 map of Harthill showing the mediaeval open field systems.

A spur was taken off Packman Lane sometime after 1720 to bring travellers across the South and Middle Fields to Harthill. One would imagine that a straight line would have made the most sense, any deviations only taking into account any major obstacles that may have stood in the way. Yet when the road approaches the area behind the Burr Well, instead of an angled deviation, the road curves. Why is that? Could it be because the road had to go around an existing feature?

Figure 23a: An aerial photograph of the modern day landscape around Loscar Farm, Harthill. Overlaid over the photograph is the hand drawn 1720 map of Harthill showing the mediaeval open field systems. Despite its details, there is no

indication of any discernible features recorded on the map, including the Burr Well.

However, by looking at the 1720, which was drawn prior to the building of the road between Packman Lane and Harthill, it can be clearly seen that the line of the road could have been laid down in a straight line. On the 1720 map, there were no woods or obstacles in its path that would have made it necessary for the road to curve as it does on Common Road, unless it was sweeping past an existing feature or obstacle. Could that obstacle have been a large enclosure?

Figure 24: Why does Common Road at Harthill (left) curve at this point in the road? Please note that evidence of the Brickwork Plan Field System can be seen running across the large circular feature in the field.

Another interesting feature that I spotted in 2006 was a large circular crop mark in the field at the road junctions of Common Road and Harthill Field Road.

128

Figure 25: A view of the whole area where three circular scars can be seen in the field between Common Road, and Harthill Field Road, Harthill. Is this evidence of a possible burh site?

I now believe that there are two, or possibly three circular enclosures in this field. The largest enclosure looks to be the oldest, with a smaller enclosure having been placed over the side of the larger enclosure at a later date. A third crescent shaped enclosure is actually on the corner of the two road junctions mentioned above. This one is much harder to see than the other two, but I believe that it was probably part of the larger enclosure rather than a later addition. It is impossible to say for certain whether or not this is indeed evidence of a possible burh.

Figure 26: Using the artist's impression of the South Creake burh, I have overlaid this representation over the area at Harthill where circular scars in the soil can be clearly seen. Was this area at Harthill the site of an iron age burh?

There is no visible evidence surviving at ground level that would identify this flat site as being the location of a possible burh site. Any possible remains have probably been destroyed by centuries of excessive ploughing. However, the name of the *'Burr Well'* is intriguing, but the discovery of a similar burh site at South Creake, in Norfolk does suggest that the site at Harthill (above) could be a similar unrecorded burh site.

Norfolk is the flattest part of the UK and yet a burh has been discovered there. The similarities of the landscape between South Creake and Harthill are remarkable. And, the discovery of this site in Norfolk led to the Norfolk Archaeological Trust buying the land to preserve this unique site for posterity before further destruction occurred from excessive ploughing.

Go to the following websites for further information about this site: http://www.norfarchtrust.org.uk/bloodgate/index.htm Also, read the descriptions of the South Creake site on the 'Megalith Portal' website at: http://www.megalithic.co.uk/article.php?sid=4806 and judge for yourself.

Figure 27: The artist's impression of the South Creake Burh, Norfolk. Did a similar site once dominate the Harthill landscape between the 'Burh Well' and Loscar Farm?

Figure 28: At Harthill, the larger enclosure shows evidence of 'Brickwork Field Patterns' extending over the NW corner of the enclosure which suggests that the enclosure could date from the Iron Age or possibly earlier and that the field system was laid over the site after it fell into disuse, possibly during the Roman occupation.

Without undertaking a field walk or a proper archaeological survey over the land between Common Road and Harthill Field Road it is impossible to say for certain whether that site is the location of a possible burh. However, the fact that

133

across the road, only a few metres away lies the *Burr Well*, may be the biggest clue of all. Perhaps this should really be spelt the *"Burh Well."*

The site of possible enclosures above the Burr Well would command good views over the area and it had an unlimited supply of fresh water rising out of the ground.

Within the larger enclosure can be seen three distinct circular features and a single oblong feature. The three circular features measure approximately 60ft in diameter. This is roughly the same size as the circular feature identified within this report at Honeysykes Farm. Is this evidence of possibly three more iron age round houses? The oblong feature is 200ft long and 41ft wide. It is impossible to say with certainty what exactly these features may be without a proper archaeological survey.

Figure 28a: The three circular features and single oblong feature, within the large circular enclosure of the possible burh site at Harthill. Is this evidence of a larger settlement area and other iron age round houses? Or, are these geological features?

The prospect of inhumation burials on all of these sites is more than likely looking at the different settlement areas in and around Loscar Farm, and judging from the extent of the massive field systems all around Loscar Farm. The

135

archaeology of this area is far from being non existent as CLP's archaeological consultants would have us believe.

To the west of the three circular enclosures across Harthill Field Road is a small rectangular feature on land belonging to Carr Farm that has been identified as being a Romano-British enclosure, within an Iron Age enclosure. This is miniscule in size when compared to the possible burh site opposite it, above the Burr Well.

Figure 29: The image in the small square is evidence from the National Monuments Records of an identified Romano-British site within a larger iron age enclosure. There is also evidence here of a Brickwork Plan field system at the foot of the black and white photograph.

The boundaries of ancient burhs can often still be traced to modern urban borough limits. This description fits Harthill's Common Road Burh exactly.

Consider the reason for the location of this possible burh

site. To the south of the site was the Northumbrian and Mercian border. Today the border is the County boundary between South Yorkshire and North Derbyshire.

This area was once real frontier territory and it was vital to have a defensive position on or near to the boundary crossing to ensure that the enemy could not wander across the boundary and steal your cattle or goods.

I believe that a defensive position was located on the site of Loscar Farm and Honeysykes Farm. These two farms currently sit either side of Packman Lane which serves as the parish boundary between Harthill and Thorpe Salvin.

From the location of the two farms, the land drops steeply south towards the border which is formed by the Bondhay Dike. This is a small flowing watercourse which many years ago was probably much different to how it is today.

Evidence of this site's connection with water can be found on the northern slopes of Packman Lane behind the two farms. Another small watercourse runs around the hill that the two farms sit on top of. And, the most obvious clue is that the Anglo-Saxon word for watercourse is *"Syke."* As in *Honeysykes* Farm.

It is possible that this hill was once partially surrounded by water when the water table was much higher? The top of this site may have seemed like an island, surrounded by water, rising defiantly above the landscape. This would have been an ideal location to look out for potential enemy tribes approaching from the south across the border at Markland Grips. It would also have been a difficult position for any possible enemy to attack.

The water that flows around Loscar and Honeysykes Farm comes from an underground source that presumably once fed the Burr Well. The water flows around the northern dip behind Loscar Farm and continues under Packman Lane around behind Honeysykes Farm.

The possible burh site at Common Road may have been a secondary defensive position, or simply just another local farmstead. Just as today, we have the farms of Honeysykes Farm, Loscar Farm, Grange Farm and Carr Farm all in close proximity to one another farming the same landscape. Another possible theory is that it may have been a burial site. We will never know for certain without proper archaeological examination of these sites.

There is evidence of a possible trackway or ditches running from the dip on the northern slopes of Loscar and Honeysykes Farms. If this was not a watercourse, could it have been an entrance into the larger burh site?

Figure 30: In this negative image of the *features* showing Common Road in the foreground with Loscar Farm, Honeysykes Farm and Bondhay Golf Course situated top left. Does the dip in the northern slope of the hill behind Loscar and Honeysykes Farms show the entrance into the possible burh site between Common Road and Harthill Field Road at Harthill? The possible route can be seen meandering into the site from the top left of this photograph. Please note that more evidence of enclosures and the Brickwork Plan Field System can be seen in the bottom left of this photograph behind Crow Wood, only a short distance away from Loscar Farm. See Fig. 30a below for a normal view of this area.

141

Figure 30a: A normal black and white view of the ditches that meander into the possible burh site at Harthill. The enclosures at bottom left can be seen more clearly.

The Common Road enclosures could also be described as being a hill fort. A hillfort is commonly used by archaeologists to describe fortified enclosures located to exploit a rise in elevation for defensive advantage. This fortification consists of one or more circular or sub-circular earth or stone ramparts, often with external ditches, following the contours of the hill. Could there be such a site at Harthill?

Beyond this definition the variation in types and periods is wide. Some were also settlements whilst others appear only to have been occupied seasonally or in times of strife. Further, many hill forts, after careful archaeological excavation, have been discovered to have been used not for military purposes, but to pen in cattle, horses, or other domesticated animals.

Hill forts are especially common across Europe. In Central Europe, hill-forts start with the late Neolithic, but are especially common in the Bronze Age Urnfield culture and in the Hallstatt culture of the early Iron Age, and were being built until the Roman conquest in many areas. Julius Caesar described the large late Iron Age hill forts he encountered during his campaigns as 'oppida'. By this time the larger ones had become more like cities than fortresses and many were assimilated as Roman towns." *Source: Wikipedia online encyclopeadia.*

Another description is of an enclosed oppidum. This was a

type of large, late Iron Age settlement, or *oppidum* surrounded by an encircling bank and ditch. They differ from hillforts through being not necessarily sited on high ground and through being permanent settlements with a strong economic function. As well as re-occupying older hillfort sites they can also be found on valley sides and next to rivers. Evidence from archaeological excavation suggests they were centres for trade, politics and religion with certain areas within the enclosure being dedicated to each function.

Other points of interest at this possible burh site can be seen below. Evidence of oblong and circular scars can be clearly seen in these photographs. The long ditches that run from Packman Lane behind Loscar Farm into this site could be the remains of an entrance or entrances into the site. Without proper investigation only a fool would assume with certainty what these features may prove to be. One can only highlight these features around Harthill and then leave it to the experts to investigate it further.

Figure 31: This photograph clearly shows evidence of ditches and circles in and around the edge of the field leading from Loscar Farm. If this was not a burh site, could it have been a ritualistic burial site? Only a proper archaeological survey and excavation will be able to say what this site was used for.

Figure 32: View looking south: The ditches that lead from the northern end of Loscar Farm into this possible burh site can be seen much clearer here. Please also note the enclosures in the foreground behind the 'tick-shaped' Crow Wood. The meandering scar created by the water that once flowed from the Burr Well can also be clearly seen at the edge of the field to the right of Crow Wood.

Figure 33: An overhead view of the possible burh site or burial site north of Loscar Farm.

Figure 33a: An overhead view of the possible burh site and its location to Loscar Farm and the village of Harthill with Woodall.

Figure 34: The field at Carr Farm where the NMR have a record of a Romano-British site within an earlier and much larger triangular shaped iron age enclosure. Please note its proximity to the possible burh or burial site.

Figure 35: A black and white photograph of the possible burh or burial site. Evidence of circular and oblong crop marks can be clearly seen. Please also note the enclosures in the centre at the foot of the photograph situated behind Crow Wood and only metres away from Loscar farmland. Were all of these nearby sites interconnected?

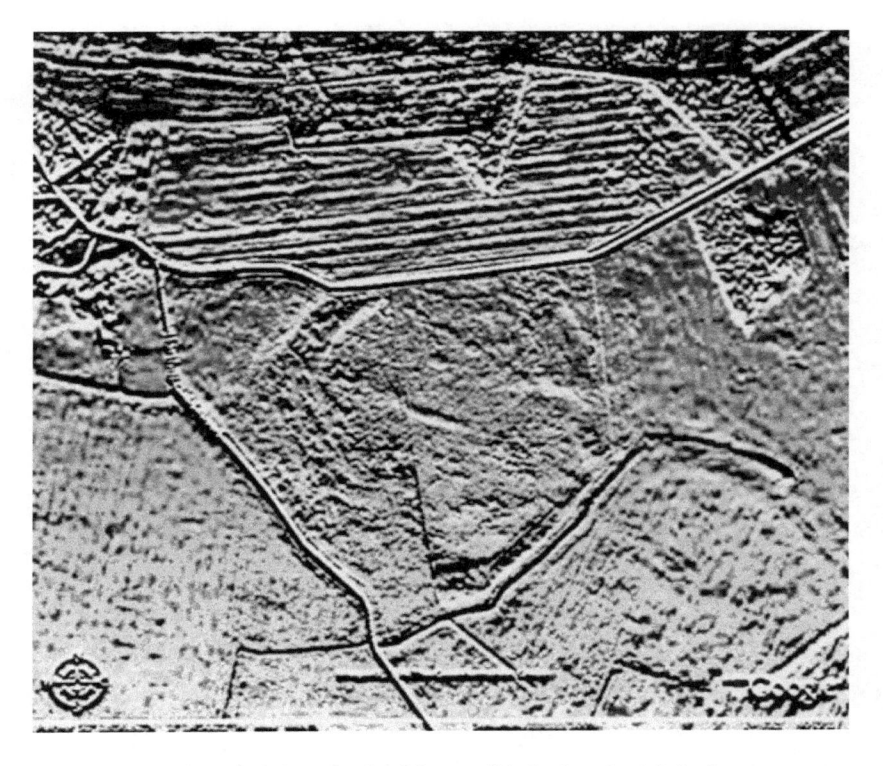

Figure 36: A bas relief photograph of the possible burh or burial site between Common Road and Harthill Field Road, Harthill.

Figure 37: A normal photograph of the possible burh or burial site between Common Road and Harthill Field Road, Harthill.

Figure 37a: Another bas relief photograph of the possible burh or burial site at Harthill showing a much wider area. This is viewed looking north and the ditches (centre right) leading from Loscar Farm can be clearly seen.

Figure 38: A wider view of the possible burh or burial site at Harthill.

Figure 39: A black and white view of the features around and within the possible burh or burial site at Harthill.

Figure 40: Evidence of enclosures and Brickwork Plan Field System behind Crow Wood, Harthill. This remarkable feature is a short distance away from the northern boundary of Loscar Farm. Over the years I have found several carved and tooled stones in the edge of the field behind Crow Wood. Several are shaped like animal heads, rabbits, dogs, deer, frog etc., some have animal heads crudely carved on them and most have more than one animal carved on each stone. In 2017 I found two more enclosures in the field side by side directly behind Crow Wood. In 2005 I found a hand-shaped curved stone across the road from this field towards Harthill Field Road. The same year I found a similar shaped stone in the field behind Crow Wood. It was not until 2017 whilst photographing these stones that I noticed that the two stones were exactly the same shape. This suggests that people were not making random objects but were making items for a specific purpose and which were scaleable in size.

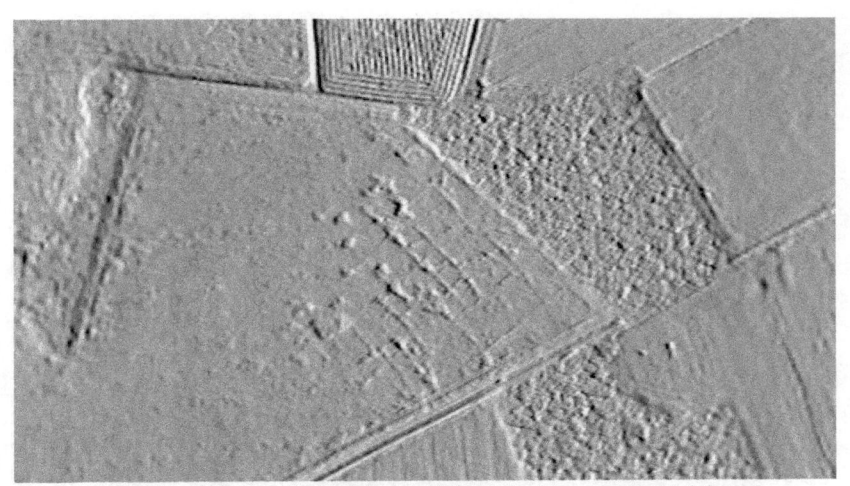

Figure 40a: Above, a bas relief view to highlight the layout of the Brickwork Plan field system and enclosures behind Crow Wood, at the side of Common Road, Harthill. Below the features sit on a low plateau in the field.

Figure 40b: A more detailed view of the enclosures and Brickwork Plan field system behind Crow Wood at the side of Common Road, Harthill.

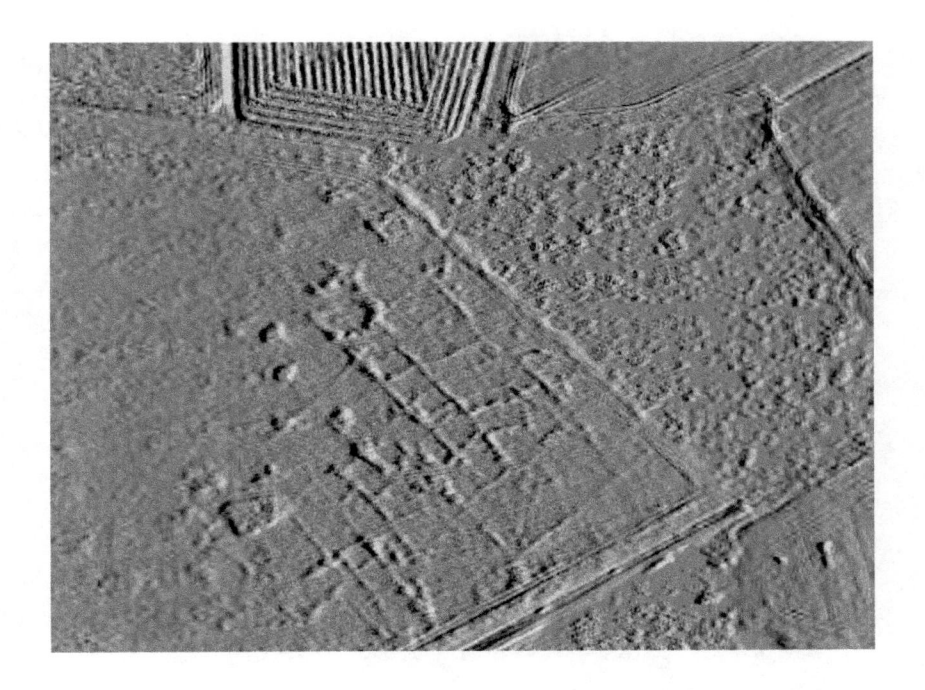

Figure 40c: A much clearer bas relief photograph of the Crow Wood field system and enclosures at the side of Common Road, Harthill.

Figure 40d: Evidence of enclosures and the Brickwork Plan field system behind Crow Wood at the side of Common Road, Harthill. This site is only 237 metres from the edge of Loscar farmland. If Npower's and CLP's archaeological consultants were indeed looking for archaeology within a 1km of the Loscar Farm site, how did they miss this site? As archaeological experts, they would have known about Google Earth as a resource that would have allowed them to scour the landscape around Loscar Farm. Google Earth, unlike the aerial photographs from the National Monuments Records is free for anyone to use.

Figure 41: Grange Farm, Harthill a short distance west of Loscar Farm showing light coloured crop marks in their fields.

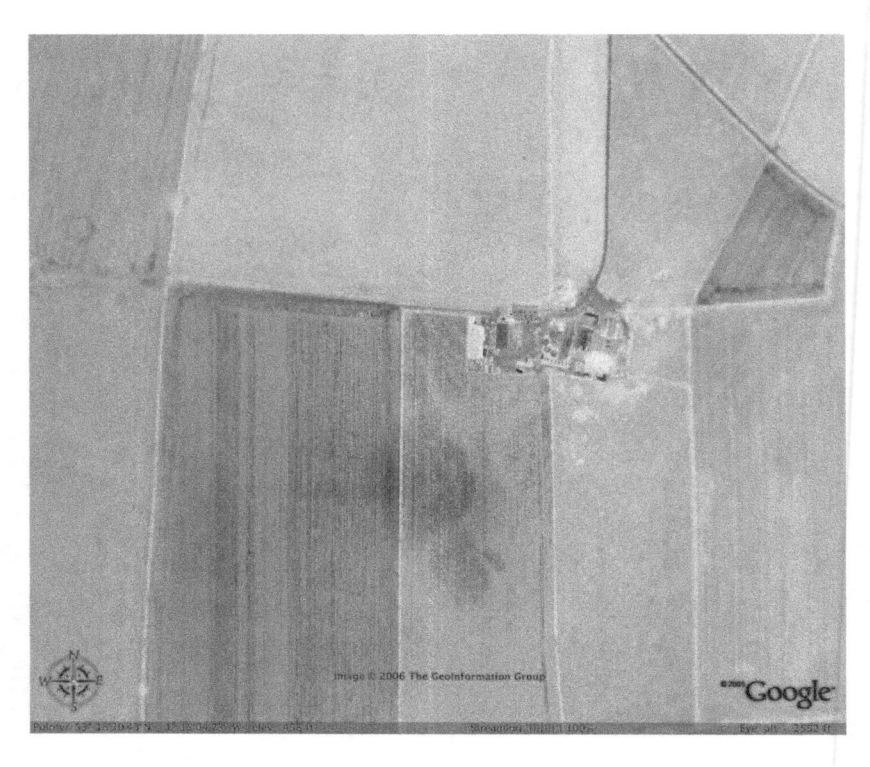

Figure 41a: A negative image of Grange Farm, Harthill.

Figure 42: View of Grange Farm, Loscar Farm and Honeysykes Farm showing the proximity of unknown archaeological features in the immediate vicinity of Loscar Farm.

Figure 43: Crop marks at Grange Farm, west of Loscar Farm, Harthill.

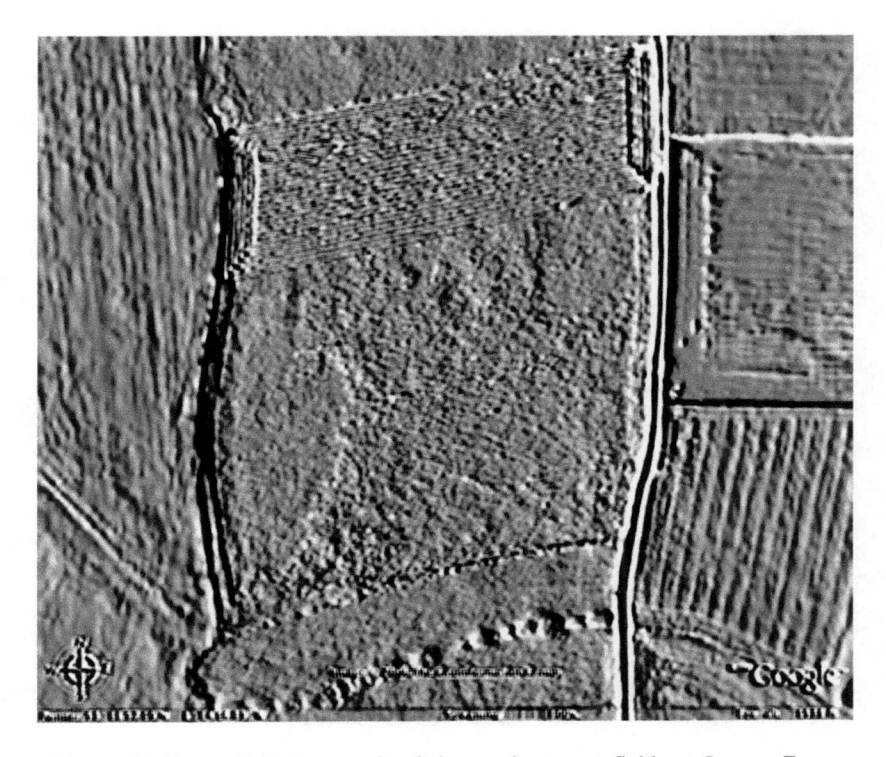

Figure 44: Bas relief photograph of the northernmost fields at Loscar Farm. Evidence of Ladder shaped enclosures can be seen in the bottom right corner of the field running diagonally in a NW direction away from Packman Lane.

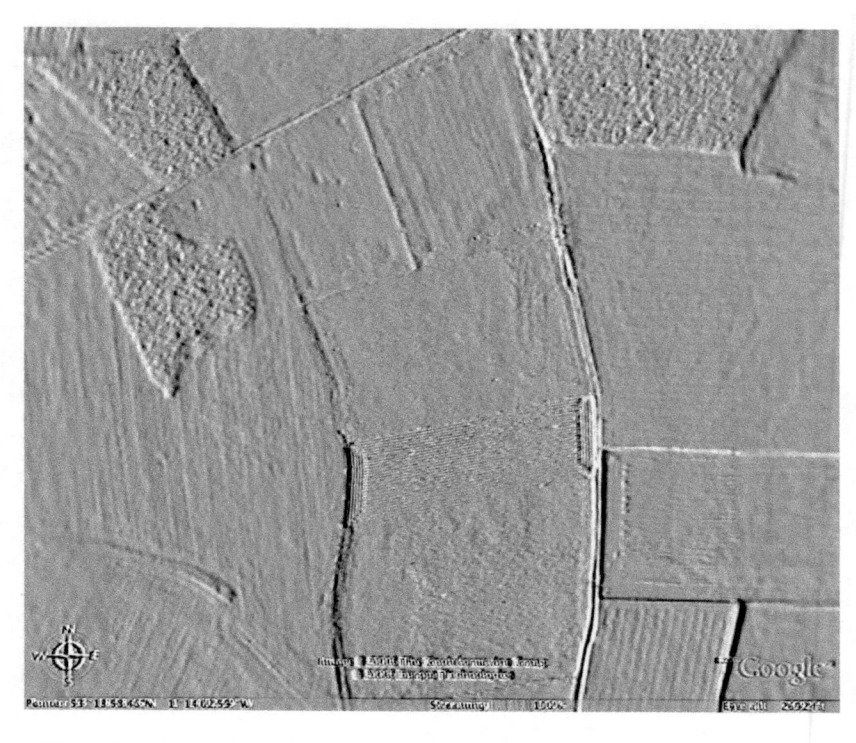

Figure 44a: Another bas relief photograph of Loscar Farm's northernmost fields. The ladder shaped enclosures can be seen just above the end of the centre text at the bottom of the photograph.

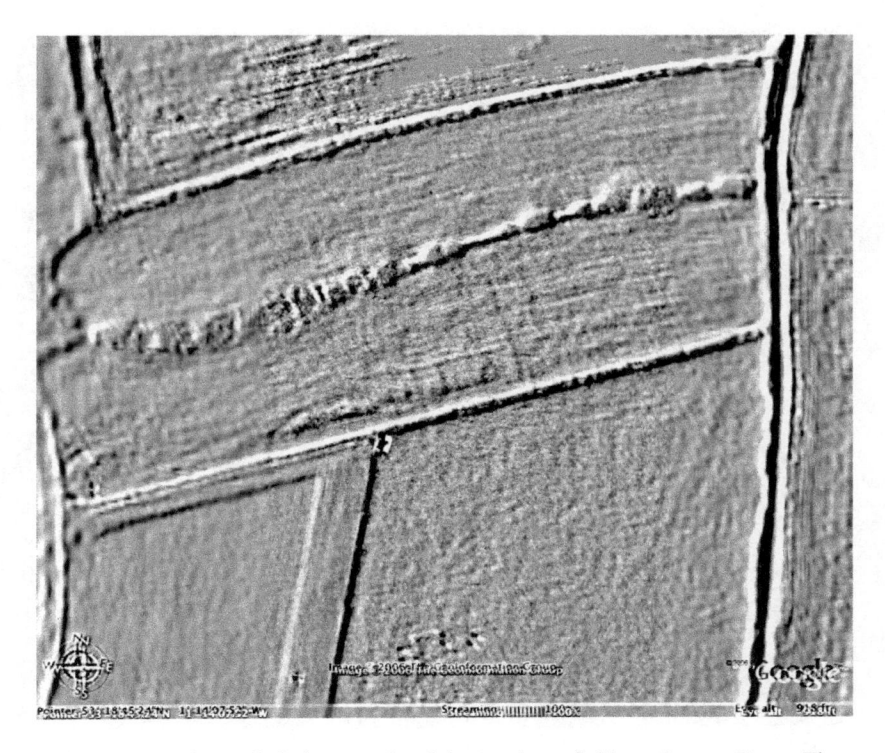

Figure 45: A bas relief photograph of the northern fields at Loscar Farm. The hedgerow running across the photograph can be found in the dip at the northern slope behind Loscar Farm. There is also evidence here of rectangular shaped enclosures running parallel along the opposite field edge below the hedgerow. A right angled shadow can also be seen running across the field joining the enclosures to the hedgerow on the opposite side of the field.

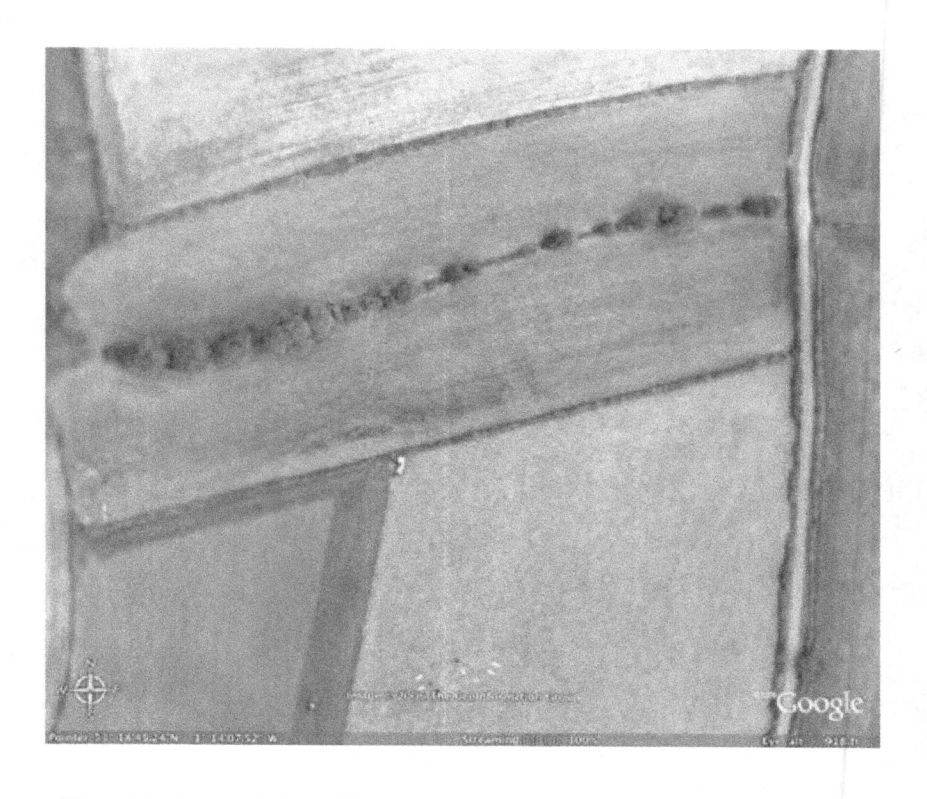

Figure 45a: A normal view of the area shown in Fig. 45. Evidence of the enclosures can be seen here.

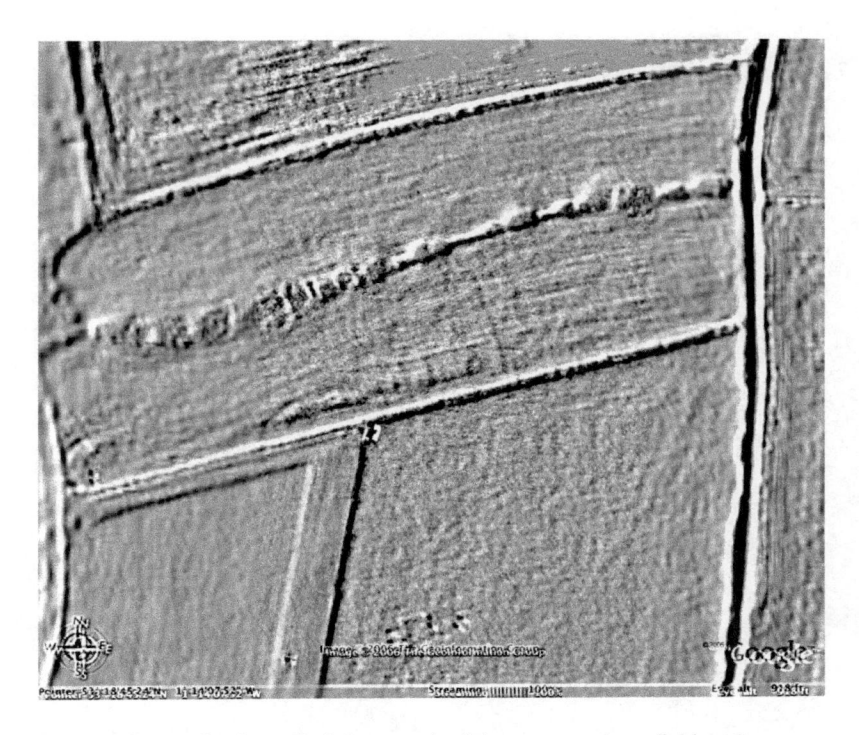

Figure 45b: Another bas relief photograph of the same northern fields at Loscar Farm. The ladder shaped enclosures can be seen more clearly in the centre of this photograph.

Figure 46: Scratta Wood, *"an important iron age settlement"* according to (Challis and Harding 1975:94) in Riley's book, Early Landscape from the air' 1980, p.70) lies only a short distance east of Honeysykes Farm. Evidence of the Brickwork Plan field system can be seen running diagonally across the enclosures.

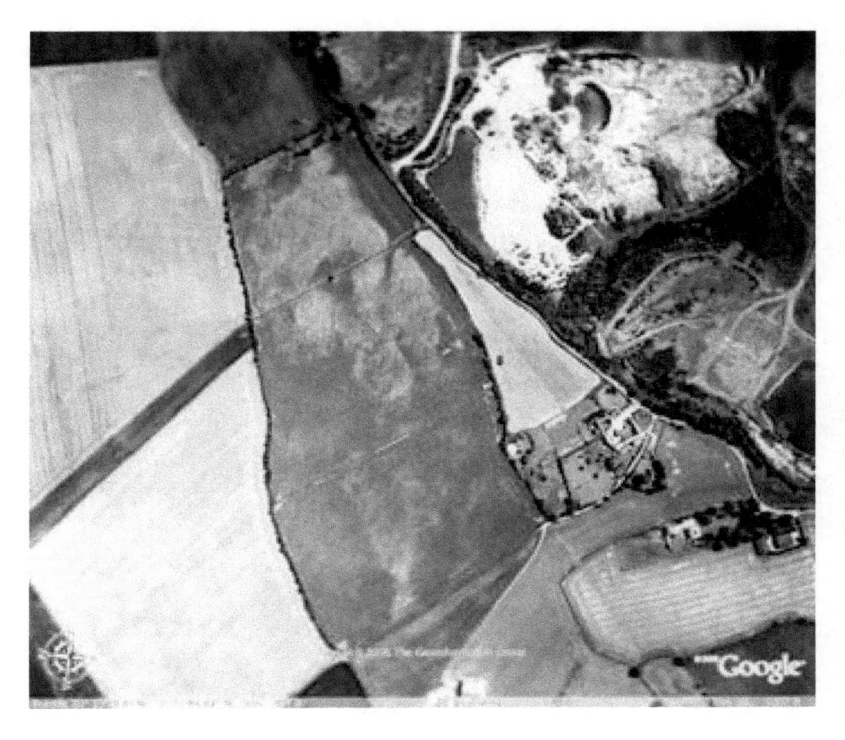

Figure 46a: A clearer black and white photograph of the "important iron age settlement" at Scratta Wood.

Figure 47: Evidence in the fields NE of Honeysykes Farm at Thorpe Salvin showing more Brickwork Plan field systems with what may be evidence that a stream once ran through it.

Figure 47a: A closer look at the field showing the complex Brickwork Plan field system can be clearly seen here.

Figure 48: This photograph shows a more detailed Nuclear Plan field system alongside the runway of the Netherthorpe Airfield at Thorpe Salvin. Ironically, D.N. Riley, who first spotted these field systems in Rossington used to fly out of Netherthorpe Airfield to carry out his aerial observations. However he did not spot this complex field system at the side of the runway that he used on a regular basis in the 1970s and 80s to carry out his study.

Figure 48a: A clearer black and white photo taken from a different angle of the Nuclear Plan field system beside the runway of Netherthorpe Airfield at Thorpe Salvin.

Figure 49: Evidence of the field plan systems south of Thorpe Salvin.

Figure 49a: The same field photographed from a different angle Showing more field plan crop marks at Thorpe Salvin.

Figure 50: Evidence of the Brickwork Plan field system in the north field of Honeysykes Farm.

Figure 51: Brickwork Plan field systems in the field east of Honeysykes Farm.

Figure 52: The complex archaeology in the south field at Honeysykes Farm.

Figure 53: View looking south of the Brickwork Plan field systems on Honeysykes farmland.

Figure 54: Carr Farm (top left) showing evidence of a possible triangular-shaped enclosure in its south field.

Figure 54a: A close up view of a possible triangular-shaped enclosure south of Carr Farm.

182

Figure 55: More evidence of the Brickwork Plan field systems in the fields across the road below Loscar Farm's south field.

Figure 56: A photo montage of the sloping, south facing, south field at Honeysykes Farm.

Tooled, shaped and decorated stone artefacts found by the author in the field close to the archaeological feature behind Crow Wood, off Common Road, Harthill.

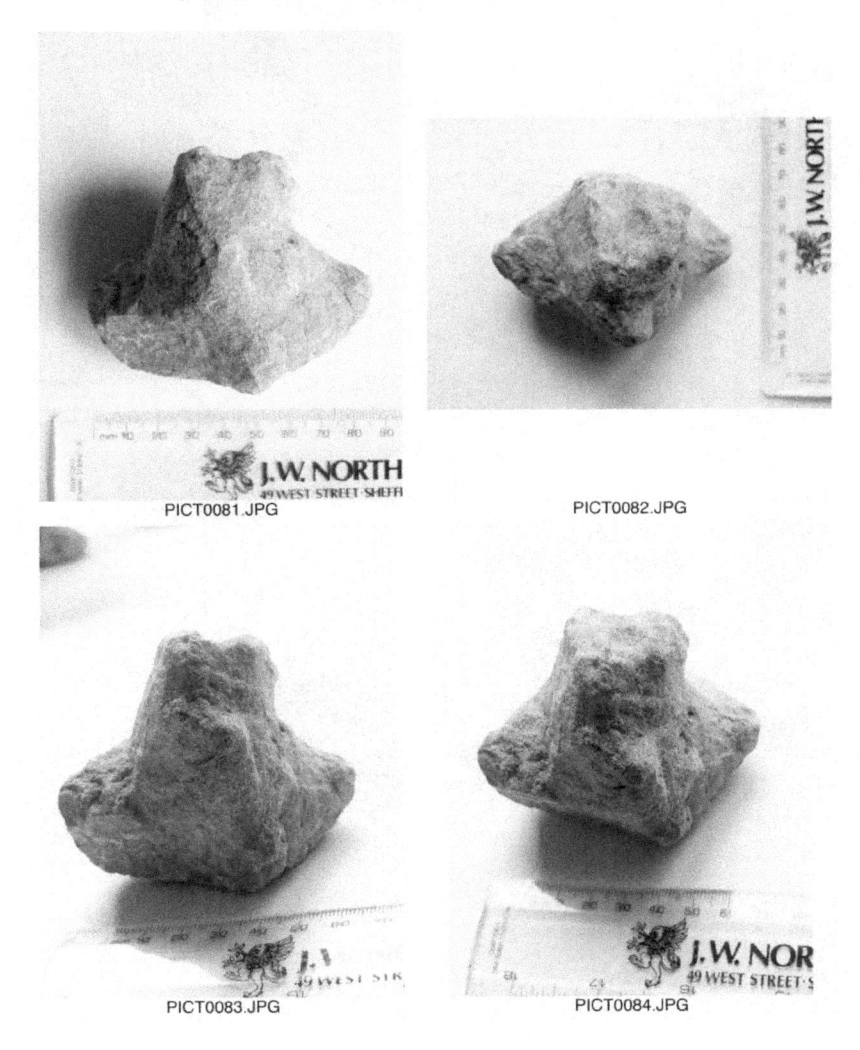

PICT0081.JPG

PICT0082.JPG

PICT0083.JPG

PICT0084.JPG

185

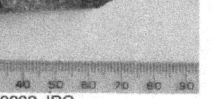

PICT0032.JPG

PICT0034.JPG

PICT0035.JPG

PICT0036.JPG

186

PICT0086.JPG

PICT0087.JPG

PICT0088.JPG

PICT0089.JPG

PICT0091.JPG

PICT0056.JPG   PICT0057.JPG   PICT0058.JPG

PICT0059.JPG   PICT0060.JPG   PICT0061.JPG

PICT0063.JPG

PICT0075.JPG

PICT0076.JPG

189

PICT0052.JPG

PICT0053.JPG

PICT0054.JPG

PICT0055.JPG

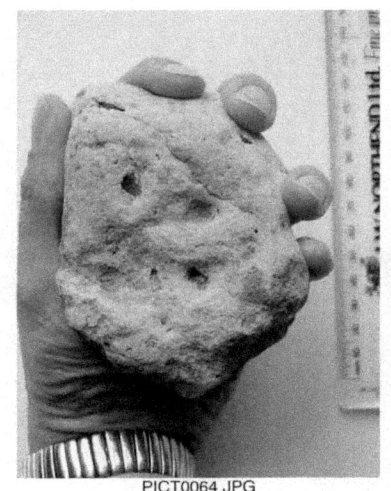

PICT0064.JPG

PICT0065.JPG

PICT0066.JPG

PICT0067.JPG

PICT0128.JPG

PICT0129.JPG

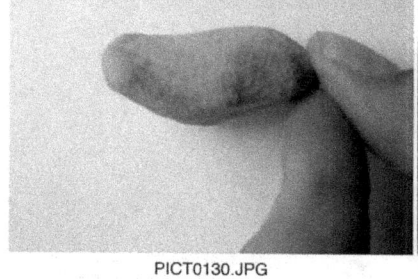

PICT0130.JPG

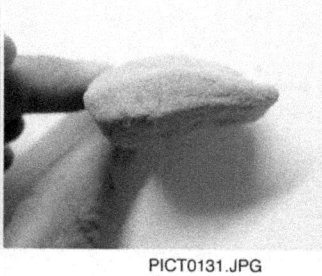

PICT0131.JPG

PICT0132.JPG

PICT0073.JPG

PICT0074.JPG

PICT0026.JPG

PICT0027.JPG

PICT0028.JPG

PICT0029.JPG

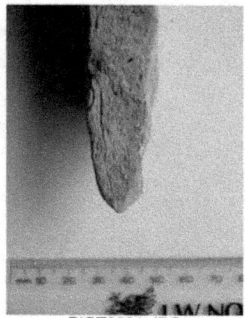

PICT0030.JPG

PICT0031.JPG

194

PICT0037.JPG

PICT0038.JPG

PICT0039.JPG

PICT0040.JPG

PICT0041.JPG

PICT0042.JPG

PICT0077.JPG

PICT0078.JPG

PICT0079.JPG

PICT0080.JPG

196

PICT0068.JPG

PICT0069.JPG

PICT0070.JPG

PICT0071.JPG

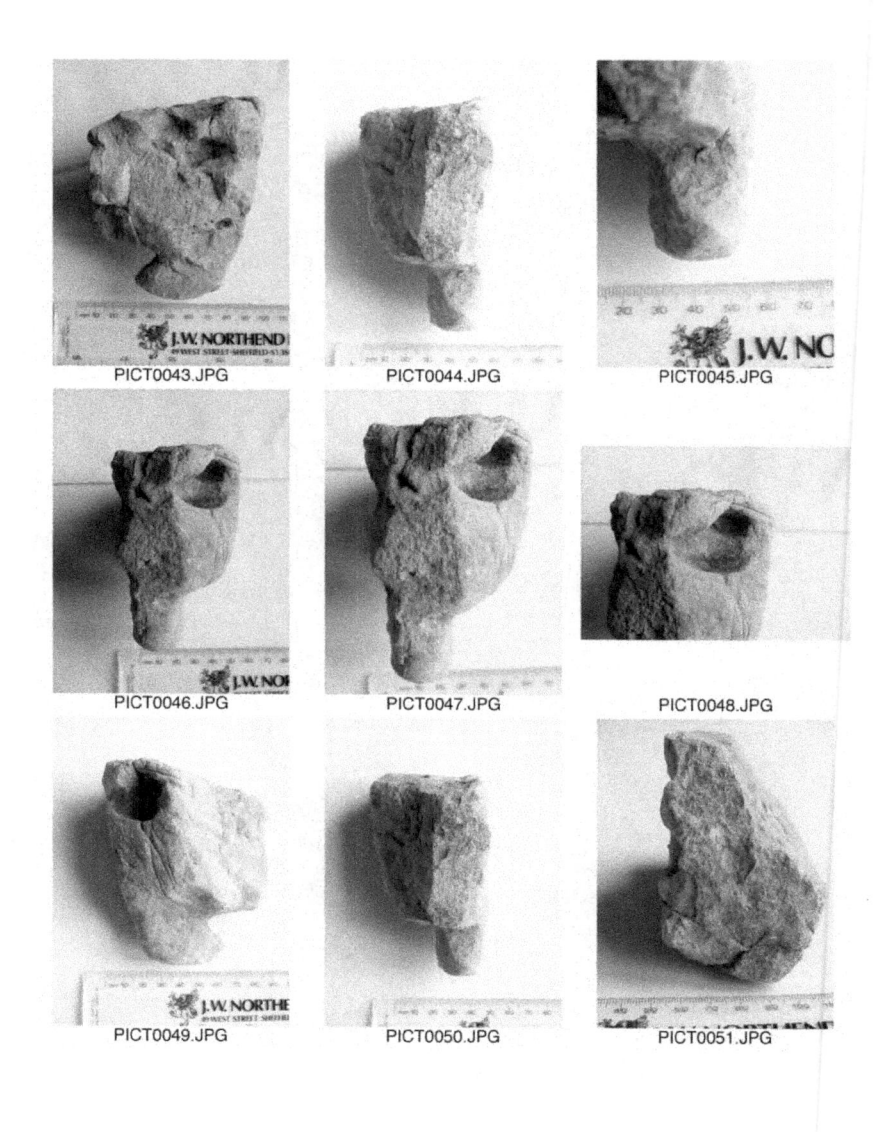

PICT0043.JPG PICT0044.JPG PICT0045.JPG

PICT0046.JPG PICT0047.JPG PICT0048.JPG

PICT0049.JPG PICT0050.JPG PICT0051.JPG

PICT0022.JPG

PICT0023.JPG

PICT0024.JPG

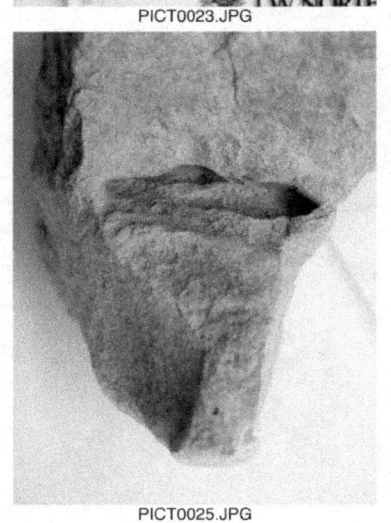

PICT0025.JPG

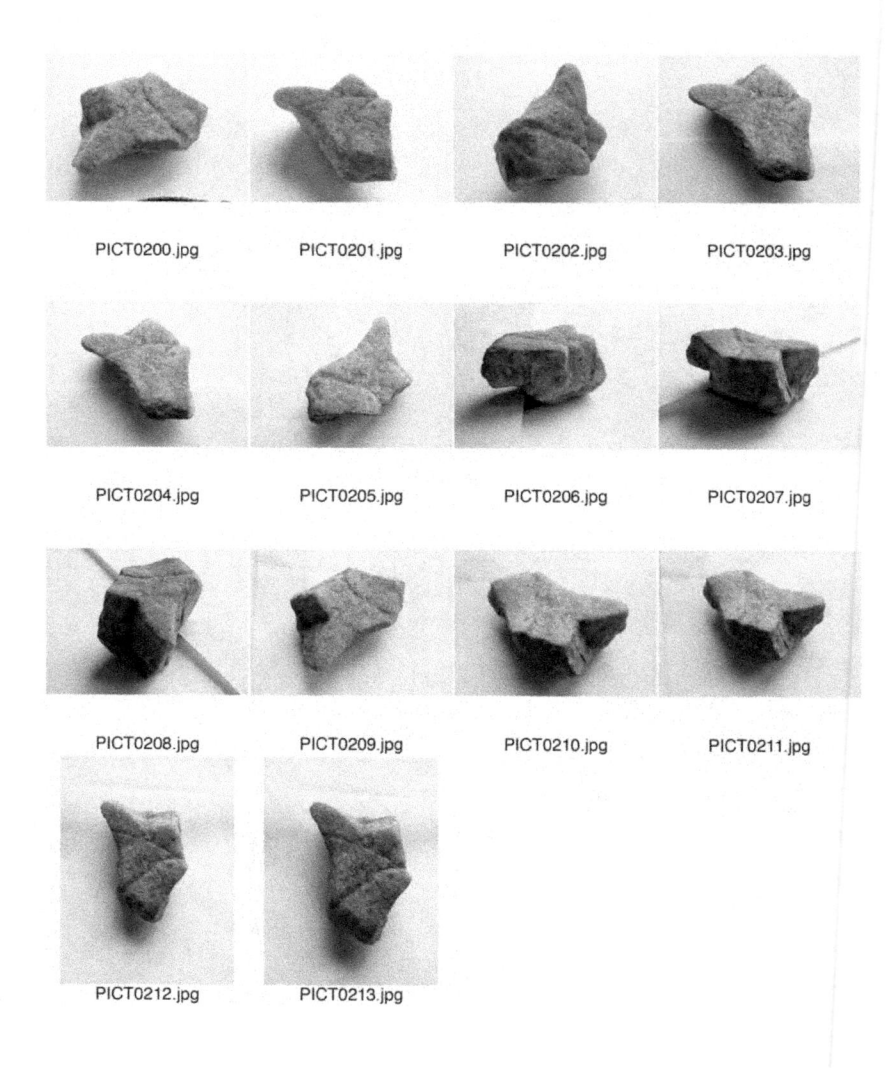

PICT0200.jpg   PICT0201.jpg   PICT0202.jpg   PICT0203.jpg

PICT0204.jpg   PICT0205.jpg   PICT0206.jpg   PICT0207.jpg

PICT0208.jpg   PICT0209.jpg   PICT0210.jpg   PICT0211.jpg

PICT0212.jpg   PICT0213.jpg

Possible Stone Carving Industry at Harthill

Below are more photographs of artefacts I have found in the fields around Harthill in 2017. I found all of these items in the edge of fields and in the woods whilst walking along footpaths or the edge of fields where locals walk everyday to exercise their dogs. Every piece was found on the surface and no item was dug out of the ground.

I believe that there was probably some kind of stone carving 'industry' going on in the fields at Harthill. The pieces I have found are crudely done and as such I think that they could be apprentice pieces or test pieces. These may date from the time Harthill Church was first being built, nearly 1,000 years ago. It's as though someone has given the carver an oddly shaped stone and said, "See what you can carve out of that?"

Above: Carved animal head. Lamb or deer?

Above: Carved deer head, photographed in situ with several other carved stones which have been ploughed out of the field and 'dumped' by the farmer at the edge of the field at Harthill. This piece was found in a cairn in Crow wood where for the last few years, locals have been picking up stones at the edge of this field and adding them to the cairn. I found three carved animal heads in this cairn.

Above: I picked this carved stone of a frog up in the wood close to the entrance on Common Road, Harthill. When the stone is turned upside down there is also a rabbit's head carved into the same stone.

Above: A large carved rabbit found in the stone cairn in Crow Wood, Harthill.

Above: A Mesolithic flint hammer head found in the fields at Harthill. There is a 3mm channel carved around the neck which is carved at a perfect right angle. There is evidence of what appears to be copper material still in the carved channel.

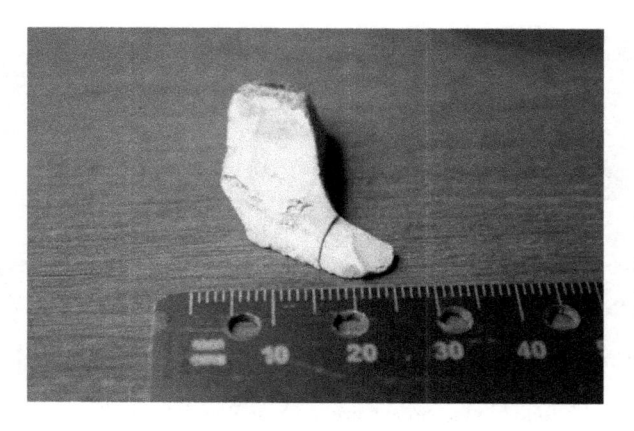

Above: A small flint tool found in the fields at Harthill.

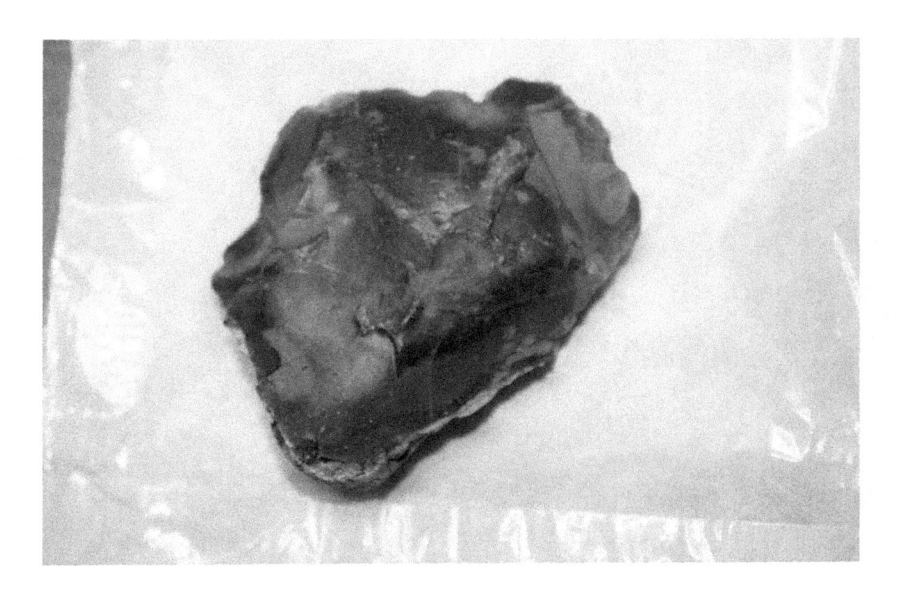

Above: Found close to the flint tool on the previous page was this piece of knapped chert which is not native to Rotherham.

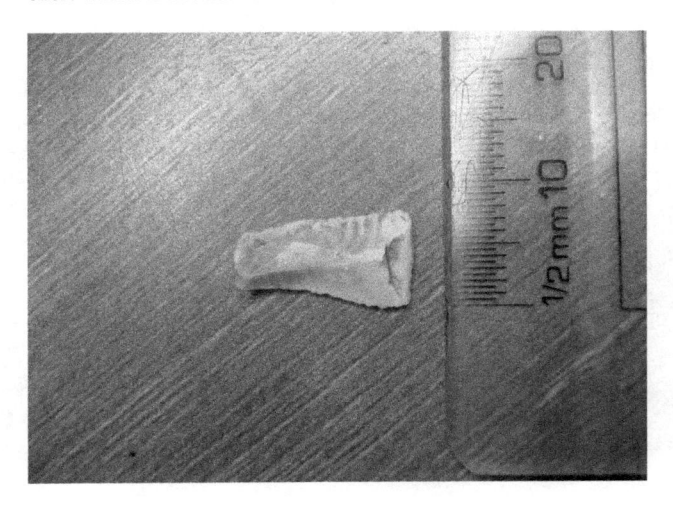

Above: A microlith found close to the flint items above at Harthill, Rotherham.

Above: This piece of fired red clay found in the fields around Harthill has three subjects modelled into it. An owl, a rabbit and this impressive warrior wearing a helm and holding a shield. The warrior's helm has stones inlaid into it. The shield also has indentations in it that must have been where stones were pushed into the clay but which probably later fell out. Below left: the Owl. Below right: the Rabbit also showing the owl in the bottom right corner.

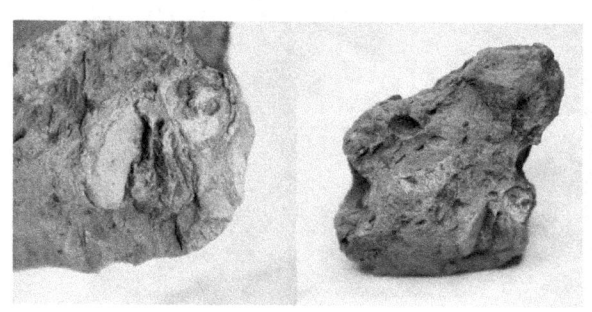

Figure 57: A map of the eastern fields around Harthill.

Figure 58: An aerial photograph taken by the author in 1992 over the south field at Loscar Farm showing Bondhay Barn on the left. Please note, that even in this photograph, evidence of hollows and dark cropmarks can be seen running at right angles from the field edge in the bottom right of this photograph. Also note the scale of the curve in the road where it bends around the roadside enclosure feature a few metres across the road from Loscar Farm on the neighbouring Honeysykes Farm land.

Figure 59: Finally, an impressive photograph of a 44 acre field at Thorpe Salvin showing huge enclosures and ditches possibly dating somewhere between the Iron Age and Romano-British period. Further archaeological investigation is required here.

The close proximity of Harthill to the north Nottinghamshire border is of interest and importance. If one looks at the East Midlands Archaeological Research Framework you can see how the archaeology in these two areas around Loscar Farm, on the South Yorkshire and north Nottinghamshire border have overlapped and are similar in many respects.

"Despite all these discoveries and excavation, there remain limitations to our knowledge about Roman sites in

Nottinghamshire. Substantial parts of the County are on geologies and soils, which do not generally produce cropmarks. Consequently, we are dependent upon the 'traditional' means of site recognition in the claylands of the Mercia Mudstones north and south of the Trent, in the Coal Measures, and to a large extent also on the Magnesian Limestone. Here, the lack of systematic fieldwork limits both knowledge and interpretation, as does the lack of reporting to the SMR of Roman finds by both finders and researchers." (East Midlands Archaeological Research Framework: Resource Assessment of Roman Nottinghamshire – *'An Archaeological Resource Assessment of Roman Nottinghamshire'* by Mike Bishop, Principal Archaeological Officer, Environment Department, Nottinghamshire County Council. p.2.)

"When all sources of information are put together, it is evident that the whole of Nottinghamshire was well settled, and its landscape well used, during the Roman period. At its apogee, probably in the 2nd and 3rd centuries A.D., its

population probably equalled, perhaps exceeded, that of 1086." (Bishop. Ibid. p.2.) The area that the Brickwork Plan field systems cover at Harthill would suggest that the population farming this land was far greater than it is today.

"Nottinghamshire north of the Trent was border country between north and south, with communications channeled into the Rossington Gap on the county boundary with Yorkshire, where a gravel ridge runs through the lowland marshes... The Rossington Gap then was a critical point at which hostile movement from the north had to be controlled. If such movement were not broken in this area, then the last line of defence between north and south was the Trent, for once this was crossed a multiplicity of routes southwards were available." (Bishop. Ibid. p.3-4.) Harthill was part of this *'critical point'* on the border, and the archaeology around Loscar Farm does suggest that it was quite extensive and complex.

"Settlement complexes similar to the types seen in the Trent Valley are also found on the west bank of the Idle Valley,

211

where they appear to be on the eastern margin of the so-called 'Brickwork Plan' landscape of the northern Sherwood Sandstones. Christened the 'brickwork plan' because of the rectilinear fields which originally appeared to be characteristic, this landscape has been shown in fact to be made up of a number of elements, phases and settlement types, with a chronological depth which begins before the Conquest and extends to the 4th century. Simple rectangular enclosures of varying sizes, with varying depths and widths of ditches, and clusters of enclosures appear to characterise the Roman phases. Excavation on one such cluster at Dunstan's Clump revealed occupation spanning the 1st to 3rd centuries, within a rectangular post-built structures. Excavation of another ditched rectangular enclosure, on the edge of another cluster, at Menagerie Wood, Worksop, showed settlement from the 2nd to 4th centuries with several phases of ditch digging, pits, post-hole, and possible palisades." (Bishop. Ibid. p.4.) It is possible that a multi-layered archaeological landscape will emerge on and around

Loscar Farm once a thorough archaeological survey has been requested by the RMBC.

"The 'Brickwork Plan' landscape covers over 100 square miles in North Nottinghamshire. Farther south on the same Sherwood Sandstones, comparable enclosures and clusters of enclosures appear with some adjacent pieces of field systems, but without the apparent extent and coherence seen in the north. Elsewhere, evidence for settlement consists largely of finds and some few excavated features. These show that, settlement was extensive in the Clays and Coal Measures and probably no less dense than in the areas producing cropmarks." (Bishop. Ibid. p.5.) The possibility to uncover large scale unknown and unrecorded archaeology in the Rotherham Metropolitan Borough is an exciting prospect. It shows the *'true'* value of this landscape!

"Many of the rectilinear fields in the 'brickwork plan' and their associated enclosures for example, appear to be infilling central areas on the Sherwood Sandstones which had been left by the occupants of the earlier settlements on

the peripheries. Such evidence may suggest that the Roman period saw an initial rise in and then maintenance of population levels until at least the 4th century, and probably later." (Bishop. Ibid. p.5.) The archaeology around Loscar Farm may provide valuable information about the use of the landscape by early man in the Harthill area. This is a landscape that has remained largely unspoilt for over 2,000 years, but which could be totally destroyed and lost forever within a few short months that it would take to build the wind turbines at Loscar Farm.

"Cremation burials are recorded at Newark, and mausolea for cremations at the Mansfield Woodhouse Villa. Inhumation burials are known from Greasley, Scrooby and from the cemeteries of the small towns of Margidunum and Brough, where lead coffins have also been produced." (Bishop. Ibid. p.7.) Looking at the extent of the archaeology around Loscar Farm, there is a great possibility of burials being found around the surrounding landscape at Loscar and Honeysykes Farms.

"In Nottinghamshire north and west of the Trent there appears to have been retraction of settlement and the eventual conversion of the sandlands to rough grazing and woodland, with huge expansion of woods on the clays of the Mercia Mudstones and the Coal Measures." (Bishop. Ibid. p.8.) The landscape around Loscar Farm may provide evidence of this change in use of the land by early man. Without a proper archaeological survey, we will never know.

"In both areas, however, some enduring influences survived. These may be seen in the continued use of some boundaries..." (Bishop. Ibid. p.2.)

This is certainly the case with the South Yorkshire/North Derbyshire/North Nottinghamshire county boundary that meet along the southern edge of Loscar and Honeysykes Farms.

The evidence of archaeology in and around Loscar Farm is plain for anyone to see. I do not need to assume anything about the evidence contained within the report because it is easy to highlight simply by using a free resource like Google

Google Earth.

Verifying what is contained within this report however, can only be done by the undertaking of a proper and thorough archaeological survey and excavations.

HARTHILL ACTION GROUP.

Response to:

Loscar Farm Wind Turbines Proposed Development.

Report compiled by The Energy Workshop Ltd for John Wilks.

ARCHAEOLOGICAL ASSESSMENT.
ADDENDUM TO PART 2.

By Paul Rowland.

On the 11th May 2005, I was approached by Mr Gerry Matthews of Harthill, whose son, Oliver was tragically killed on Packman Lane, last year by a hit-and- run driver.

Mr Matthews and his family have planted flowers and a 'Monkey Puzzle' tree in the field where their son was killed as a memorial to him. Mr Matthews informed me that Mr Wilks had telephoned him with regard to Npower's proposed widening, strengthening and realignment of Packman Lane.

Mr Wilks told Mr Matthews that he would ensure that the area where the Matthews family have planted the tree and flowers to their son's memory would not be touched by Npower as they only planned to alter the bottom end of Packman Lane. (This is interesting because in their report Npower have not specified exactly where along Packman Lane that they are planning to alter).

Mr Wilks also promised Mr Matthews that he will ensure that he receives confirmation regards their son's 'plot' in writing from Npower that they will not touch that area along Packman Lane!

Mr Matthews very kindly took me down to the field where the tree to his son's memory was planted. He told me how it took a group of them an hour and a half to dig a hole to plant the 6ft tree.

Mr Matthews who waters the tree daily then proceeded to show me what happened when he actually watered the tree. The water simply sat on the surface and took an age to soak in. This obviously proves how compacted the subsoil in the field   is. This is puzzling, for a field where crops have been grown since anyone can remember, and where, until their son's accident the farmer used to plough right up to that area.

In a conversation with the former owner of the field, Mr Mark White, he too attested to the fact that water used to always stand on top of the field along that edge. Roman roads were well constructed roads that were well compacted with rock and soil, and this would certainly be one reason why water always sits on the surface of this field.

Mr Matthews showed me the stones that they had dug out of the hole where they had planted their tree. The stones had been placed in the hedgerow bottom. There were 5 limestone 'cobbles' approximately 4 inches square. I noticed several more, all of a similar shape and size around the edge of the field. I have gathered together the loose 'cobbles' that Mr Matthews and his family dug up and a photograph of them is enclosed with this addendum.

It is not natural for limestone to be formed in 4 inch square 'cobbles'. The 'cobbles' are definitely dressed stone. They are crudely dressed stone, but they are dressed nevertheless. The quantity and shape of these stones along the edge of that field attests to the fact that these 'cobbles' are worth further archaeological investigation. The evidence does suggest that they were part of a road surface and not a wall as they are too small in size to have formed part of a wall.

Today, (12th May 2005) I found a 'cobble' in the soil of the field in question. I scraped back the soil covering it and noticed that there was another 'cobble' next to that one, and another next to that one! I have photographed these in situ and copies are attached to this addendum.

In a conversation with an archaeologist friend he informed me that only Roman roads of some importance were dressed with 'cobbles'. These were made for the rapid movement of troops, messages and supplies. I took a 'cobble' to show my friend and he confirmed that the stone was definitely a 'dressed cobble'!

Before you simply dismiss these stones as possibly nothing more than 18th to 20th century cobblestones that made up the current road I should point out that the 'cobbles' I have found, are located 3 to 4 foot to the right of the current road and lie in the soil, 3 to 4 foot below the surface of the current road surface, in the field!

The following may help to give you an idea of how big a Roman road was;

"Imagine flat, wooded virgin territory between two hilltop sighting points requiring a straight 30 foot wide roadway to be constructed upon it.

Firstly, the woodland would have to be cleared by chopping down and burning to a width of at least 90 feet. Then parallel outer ditches would be ploughed, say 90 feet apart, at the edges of the clearing. Thus would the road zone be defined and marked out initially. Then the same plough would mark out the road proper in the centre of the zone perhaps by ditches 30 feet apart, though this could vary from 15 feet to 50 feet. An embankment would be built up between the two centre ditches using material from a scoop-ditch, leaving a wide depression   along one or both sides of the road, which later traffic might travel along and wear deeper into a hollow way. On top of that a foundation of local large stones would be laid, followed by smaller stones, flints or gravel, well cambered to give good drainage, called the 'road metal' or 'metalling'.

The road embankment used to be known as the 'causeway' but is now usually described by the latin name 'Agger'. Covered with later topsoil it appears as a hump varying from a few inches in height to several feet. Together with dykes, ditches and boundary banks it comes under the general classification of 'linear earthworks.'" 'Notes to Roman Roads' by Richard W. Bagshawe. Published by Shire Publications Ltd. First printed 1979.

The current width of Packman Lane is approximately 3 metres (9ft wide). At its smallest known and recorded size, the Roman road would still be 6 foot wider than Packman Lane, and one may be lying undiscovered in the fields adjacent to Packman Lane.

On the evidence presented here, I suggest that the 'cobbles' are not a natural feature, and that their position away from the road can not possibly be part of an 18th to 20th century road surface or wall.

Thorough archaeological investigations are needed along Packman Lane to ascertain whether or not the 'cobbles' that the Matthews family have unearthed are in fact part of the ancient Roman road, known locally for centuries as Ryknild Street.

If the 'cobbles' are found to be part of a Roman road, then further investigation will be needed to identify where the road was going to, and from. It will also highlight the need for a much wider archaeological survey of the surrounding fields, and I hope that it will prevent the Lane from being damaged beyond all recognition forever by Npower Renewables.

Dressed cobblestone 4 inches square unearthed in field, SK509813, Packman Lane, Harthill.

More cobbles dug out of the field SK509813 along Packman Lane, Harthill by the Matthews family.

Position of the tree in relation to Packman Lane SK509813 where the limestone cobbles were unearthed.

Another 4 inch square limestone cobble found in the edge of the field SK509813. Packman Lane, Harthill.

More 4 inch cobbles found in field at SK509813, Packman Lane, Harthill.

4 cobbles unearthed in situ, in the field SK509813, Packman Lane, Harthill by Paul Rowland (12th May 2005).

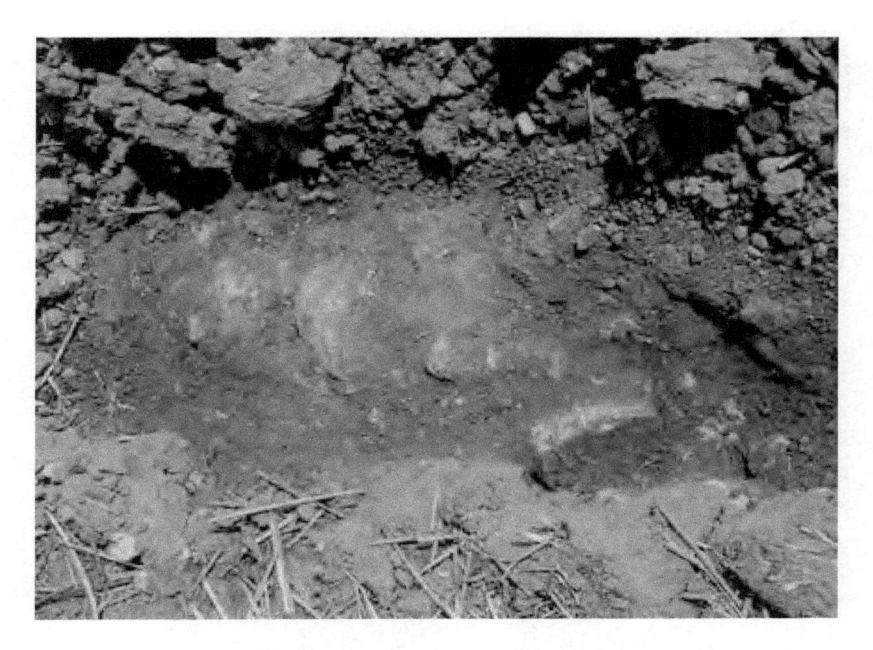

Same group of 'cobbles' with more soil scraped away to reveal more limestone'cobbles' all in situ, in the field SK509813 unearthed by Paul Rowland on 12th May 2005.

Collection of cobbles taken from the field SK509813, Packman Lane, Harthill.

Same group of cobbles in situ unearthed in field SK509813.
Packman Lane, Harthill by Paul Rowland (12th May 2005).

CARR FARM ENCLOSURES AND THE COLLECTION OF ROMAN SILVER DENARII COINS FOUND AT CARR FARM, HARTHILL.

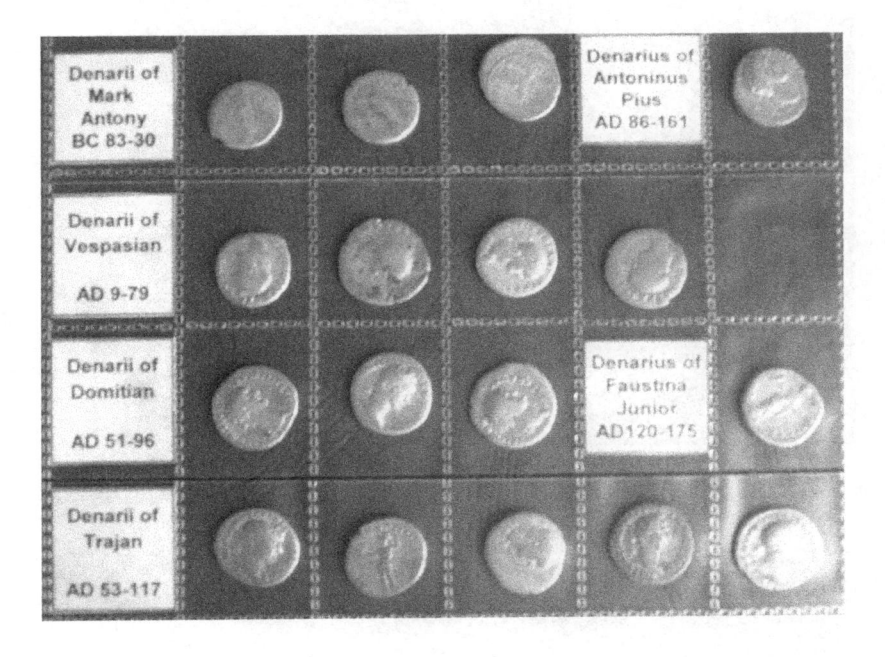

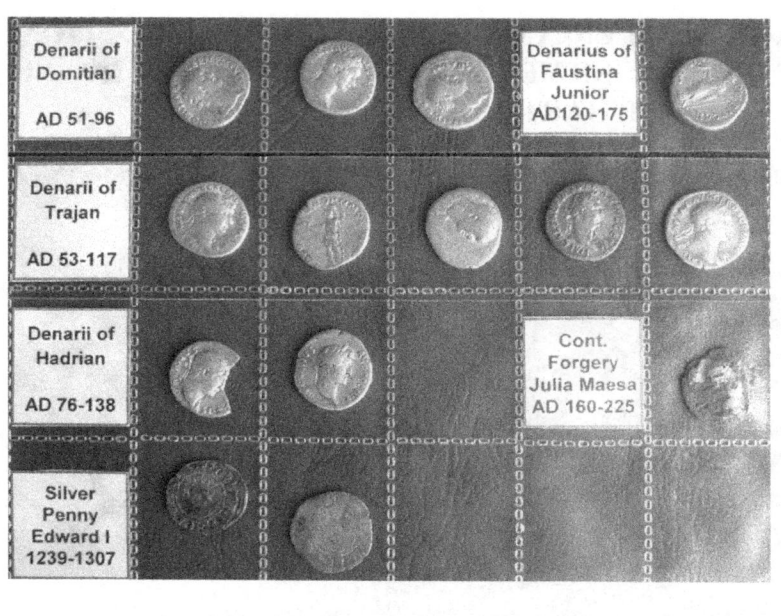

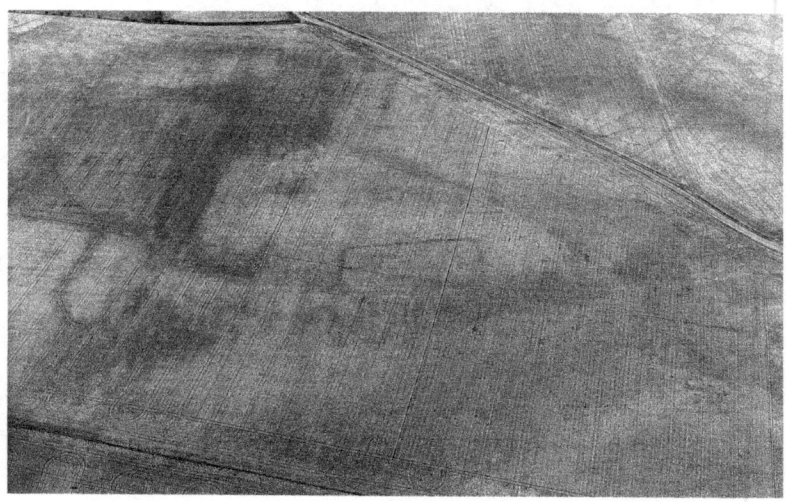

SK 4979 Photographed 5th Aug.1981. Crown Copyright. NMR. Riley Collection.

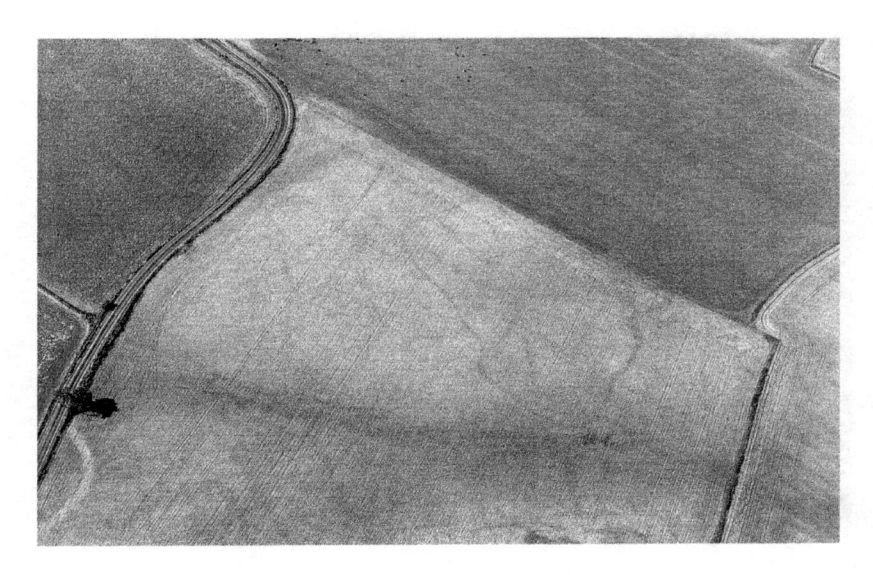

SK 4978/7 Photographed 30th Jul.1981. Crown Copyright. NMR. Riley Collection.

SK 4979/1 Photographed 30th Jul.1981. Crown Copyright. NMR. Riley Collection.

SK 4979/3 Photographed 5th Aug.1981. Crown Copyright. NMR. Riley Collection.

An enameled heraldic shaped shield stud believed to have fallen off a horse's leather harness was also found on Carr Farm Land bearing the Arms of Sir Hugh De Courtenay (1303-1377), 10th Earl of Devon.

Enameled heraldic shield shaped stud bearing the Arms of Sir Hugh De Courtenay (1303-1377), 10th Earl of Devon

Archaeological features surrounding Harthill with Woodall, South Yorkshire.

Copyright 2006. Drawn by Paul Rowland. Possible evidence of Brickwork and Nucleated Field Patterns, two Roman camps and an Iron Age Settlement?

TRANSACTIONS

OF

The Hunter Archæological Society

Vol. IX, Part 3. 1967.

SHEFFIELD:

PRINTED BY J. W. NORTHEND LTD., WEST STREET

1967

ROMAN REMAINS FROM SOUTH YORKSHIRE AND
NORTH-EAST DERBYSHIRE

By J. RADLEY and M. PLANT

SOUTH YORKSHIRE, with its Roman fort at Templeborough and its associated road system is well known to students of the Roman period, and the history of the conquest of the region has been summarised by Bartlett,[1] but hitherto no attempt has been made to survey the lesser military and civilian remains around and to the east of Sheffield. The discovery of two groups of pottery at Kiveton Park and Aston has prompted an examination of the numerous isolated finds in scattered references, in unpublished museum collections, and in private hands. It is apparent that both the sandstone area of the Rother and Sheaf Valleys and the limestone ridge to the east have a thin spread of small Romano-British occupation sites for much of the Roman period, although no farms of villa status have been found, even though they are known to the north, east and south.

EARLY MILITARY POTTERY FROM KIVETON PARK

Three hundred yards N. of Kiveton Park Station (SK 507828) behind the Station Hotel, land adjacent to Whin Covert has been stripped of its over-burden by bulldozers prior to the advance of a nearby limestone quarry face. The area, at 350' O.D. slopes south towards the Kiveton gorge and represents a terrace 50' above the valley bottom, backed by a slight rise which gives protection from northerly winds. As part of a programme of archaeological field work, the stripped area was searched for prehistoric remains, which led to the discovery of a scatter of Roman sherds. It seems likely that these sherds are the remains of a site which was partly destroyed by ploughing and wholly removed by bulldozing, save for a small patch of charcoal-rich soil. This was excavated and proved to be a hollow in the otherwise smooth rock surface.[2]

Fig. 2 shows the area which yielded the pottery. The subsoil has been churned by the bulldozers but an oval hollow 8' long, 3' wide, and 1' deep could be discerned. It was bounded on one side by the footings of a drystone wall, and was lined with small stones and cobbles which had been reddened and cracked by heat. The hollow appears to be a deliberate feature, with a stone-lined channel leading away to the east. It seems highly probable that this represents some form of kiln or oven, sunk into the ground to permit a superstructure to be erected over it at ground level. The most common type of kiln is the corn-drying kiln in which corn was parched. Whilst late Roman forms are T-shaped,[3] early drying kilns are simple

---

1 Bartlett, J. E., in Sheffield and its Region, *B.A. Handbook*, 1956, 115-20.
2 The excavation was done by R. Carr, A. Miller, and the writers in November, 1966. The bones have been examined by C. Simms, Yorkshire Museum, York; and the pottery was kindly examined by B. Hartley, University of Leeds.
3 e.g. Langtoft. Mortimer, J. R., "40 years researches . . . . ", 1905, 314-3, Fig. 1003.

linear structures as found at Elmswell.[4] This was a shallow clay-lined trench 6' long and 2' wide acting as furnace and flue, and dating at the latest to 120 A.D. This simple structure may well be the same as the hearth and channel at Kiveton Park.

After the kiln was abandoned the hollow was filled with ash, bones and pottery which after leaching and compaction formed a layer 3" thick, extending beyond the hollow to the west, and probably much further originally. Trial holes on all sides failed to reveal any other trace of structures or domestic refuse.

The kiln held a large number of shattered pot-boilers, besides large lumps of charcoal, burnt and unburnt animal bones and teeth, fragments of oyster shell, lumps of burnt clay, and pottery. Eleven teeth have been identified as pig, sheep or goat, dog or fox, and red and roe deer. The burnt clay may be derived from the kiln structure. The sherds from one vessel were sometimes grouped, and are represented as such in Fig. 2. Where observed, all the bases were upside down, as if deliberately dropped there.

The inventory of pottery below lists the main types of vessels and fabrics present, based on about 700 sherds representing at least 20 vessels, mostly jars, but including one or two bowls, beakers, platters and a flagon. Besides those illustrated (Figs. 3 and 4) there are four bases and many body sherds of grey sandy ware which in part may belong to the illustrated vessels, and 31 pieces of rustic grey ware.

The evidence for dating is based mainly on a comparison of the pottery types from early auxiliary forts and particularly from Ilkley and Slack.[5] The rare, thick, grey ware with everted and double bead rim (Fig. 3.1), the black-burnished platters with inturned rims (Fig. 4, 9 and 10) and the thin, black, sandy ware with pronounced rim and lattice-decorated body (Fig. 4.13), are found in early military contexts at Slack and Ilkley. Similarly, the rustic ware has essentially an early military distribution, occurring at Templeborough, Doncaster, Pentrich and Little Chester.[6] Curiously absent from the Kiveton Park assemblage are mortaria and Samian. The evidence points to a Roman military context in a period restricted to 80-130 A.D. — The large calcite gritted jars (Fig. 4, 7 and 11) are very well turned and fired and can here be dated by association to an early Roman rather than an early native origin.

Mr. Brian Hartley has suggested that a likely context for such a deposit of pottery would be a small *vicus* attached to a temporary military

4 Corder, P., Excavations at Elmswell, 1938, 1940, 12-13.
5 Woodward, A. M., The Roman Fort at Ilkley, *Y.A.J.* XXVII, 1926, 137-321. Dodd, P. W. and Woodward, A. M., Excavations at Slack 1913-15, *Y.A.J.* XXVI, 1922, 1-92. Gillam, J. P., Types of Roman Coarse Pottery Vessels in Northern Britain, *Arch. Ael.* XXXV, 4th Series, 1957, Article XV.
6 Thompson, F. H., The Distribution of Rustic Ware in Great Britain, *Ant. Jnl.* XXXVIII, 1958, 34.
Webster, G., *D.A.J.* LXXXI, 1961, Fig. 10, 13.
Kay, S. O., *D.A.J.* LXXXI, 1961, 139-41.

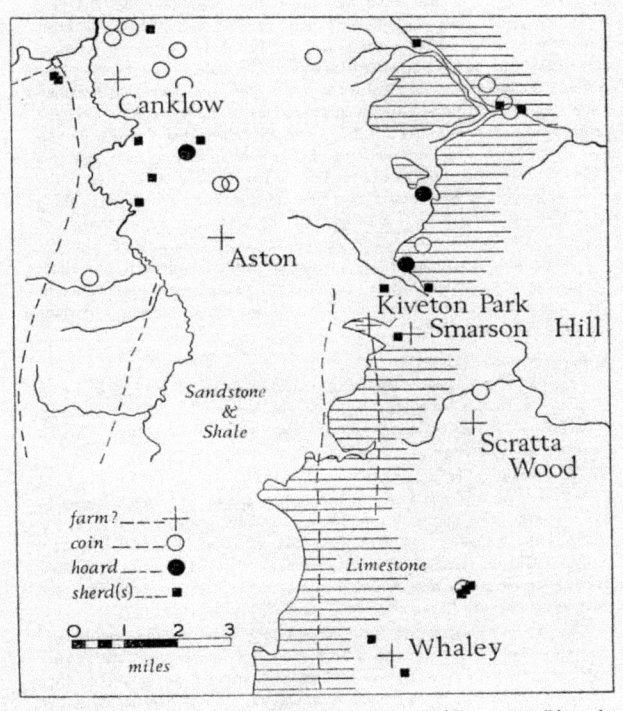

Fɪɢ. 1.—Roman remains east of the River Rother. The dashed lines are possible roads.

site. The limestone hill, on which the pottery was found, is ideally placed to have been a military site. It has been argued that a Roman road, Ryknield Street or some lesser ancient road may have followed the Magnesian Limestone exposure as far north as Kiveton Park.[7] The names Streethouse and Rikenildthorpe have been used as supporting evidence for this road line. A Gas Board trench cut in 1960 at the junction of Moor Lane and Packman Lane (SK 80858230) revealed a road surface of large, regular quartzite pebbles beneath 3' of valley silt. Local residents claim that a similar section was seen when a goal-post was erected on a nearby playing field. It seems highly probable that some sort of road did follow this line. After crossing the Kiveton gorge, the road would have to climb the first hill before changing its alignment to get to Templeborough or Doncaster. The change of alignment would take place where the military camp is postulated.

Some form of settlement may have continued here in later Roman times because on the high ground 140 yards north-west of the kiln a scatter of sherds and bones have been found on the bulldozed surface, and these include Derbyshire ware.

A ROMANO-BRITISH SITE AT ASTON

Sherds found at Aston are more typical of the small sites to be found in this area. In this instance, the sherds may represent activity in the form of a homestead, approximately on the line which a road from Kiveton Park to Templeborough would have to take.

A bungalow, "Iona", on Aughton Lane, Aston (SK 463858) was built in 1957 and pottery was found in the garden and on the bank adjacent to the pavement. The site, on Carboniferous Sandstone, is at 300' O.D. at the head of a shallow valley leading north to Ulley Brook and in a fairly sheltered position. Digging yielded 66 sherds from a few square yards, and their distribution suggested that the main part of the site was removed when the road was made over 30 years ago.[8]

Thirty-seven sherds of hard, sandy grey ware include one lattice-decorated sherd and 2 rims, and 18 sherds of thin, powdery, and soapy-textured grey ware probably belonged to one carinated jar or beaker. Five sherds of Derbyshire ware include a type A rim. Softer dark sandy native wares are represented by a few red-brown sherds. The whole assemblage could be late 1st century to late 2nd century, and is probably the remains of a small homestead.

THE SOUTH YORKSHIRE AREA IN THE ROMAN PERIOD

There are very few remains which can be called evidence of a settlement, but the scatter of small finds throughout the region is indicative of a thin

7 Hunter J., 1828, South Yorks. I, vii, 139, 309. It is called an "ancient road", with all the name forms in Smith, J., Place Names of the West Riding, 1961, 1, 151. Recently discussed by Penny, S., D.A.J. LXXXVI, 1966, 83.
8 The discovery and collection of the sherds was made by P. Mellars and J. Radley in 1957.

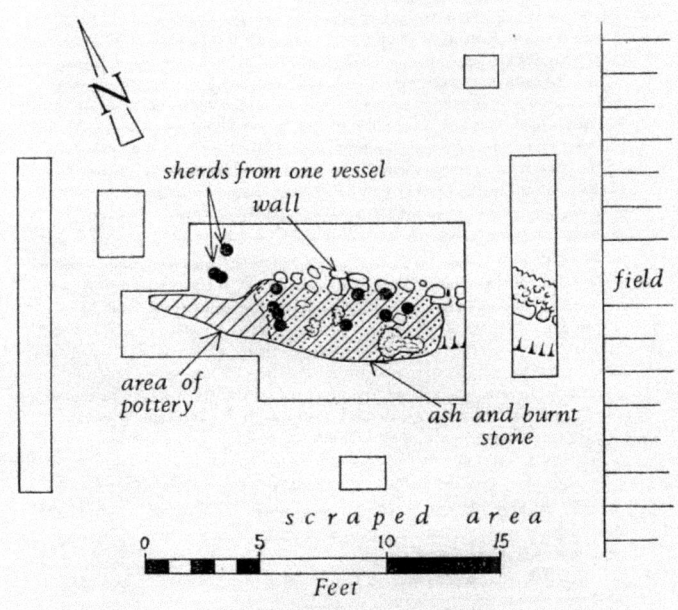

FIG. 2.—Excavated remains at Kiveton Park.

but persistent population throughout the Roman period. In the following survey, the area will be examined from west to east, beginning with the sandstone area around Sheffield and Rotherham and then the limestone area to the east, including adjacent parts of Derbyshire.

In the Sheffield area, there are some groups of finds which probably represent the remains of small homesteads. At Fulwood (SK 298853), sherds of coarse wares, predominantly Derbyshire Ware and one Dales Ware rim, and 4 bee-hive querns have been found.[9] At least 3 vessels are represented in a group of sherds of grey ware which have been found at Scott Road (SK363894),[10] and at Roe Wood 40 sherds, including grey wares, a Samian base, and a rim of a white mortarium (SK 35901)[11] have been found. Sherds were also found in the fill of the ditch of Wincobank hill-fort,[12] and querns, mostly upper stones of bee-hive querns, are recorded from Firth Park, Norton, Pitsmoor, Psalter Lane, and Wincobank.[13] Isolated sherds include a piece of Samian from Sheffield Castle excavations of 1927-9.[14]

Coin hoards have been found at Blackburn (19 coins including Domitian, Hadrian and Antoninus Pius, with a brooch),[15] Crooksmoor (30-40 coins from Decius to Tetricus),[16] Hall Carr (48 silver coins from Vitellius to M. Aurelius),[17] Scott Road (35 silver coins from Vitellius to M. Aurelius),[18] and Wybourn (100 coins from Mark Anthony to Crispina), [19] probably representing unsettled conditions in the mid 2nd century and mid 3rd century. Isolated coins have been found at Attercliffe (Constans),[20] Brightside (Magnentius),[21] Burngreave Road(Trajan Decius),[22] Crosspool(Magnentius)[23] and Tom Lane (Constantine).[24] Others on record are: Gleadless (Tacitus),[25] Wisewood (Constantine),[26] Wincobank (Vespasian and Constantius Chlorus),[27] Longley (Maximianus),[28] Shiregreen (Trajan),[29] and Woodseats (Gallienus).[30] From the outskirts of Sheffield coins have been found at Dronfield (Drusus

9 Y.A.J. XLI, 10.
10 Sheffield City Museum, J. 1906. 60.
11 Sheffield City Museum, J. 1922. 20, 75.
12 MS. report, in Sheffield City Museum; also J. 1899. 17.
13 Hunter Archaeological Index.
14 Y.A.J. XXXIX, 329; burial urns, said to be Roman and from Bank Street, Leader R. E. Guest, J., History of Rotherham, 1879, p. 605.
15 Hunter Arch. Index.
16 Hunter Arch. Index.
17 Hunter Arch. Index.
18 Rel. XXV, 1884-5, 175.
19 Gents. Mag., 1854, 490 (by S. Mitchell).
20 Hunter Arch. Index.
21 Hunter Arch. Index.
22 Y.A.J. XXXVII, 429.
23 Hunter Arch. Index.
24 Y.A.J. XLI, 10.
25 Hunter Arch. Index.
26 Hunter Arch. Index.
27 Hunter Arch. Index.
28 Hunter Arch. Index.
29 Y.A.J. XXXVII, 527. Coins, now lost, were also found at Upperthorpe. S. O. Addy, Hall of Waltheof, 1893, 18-21.
30 Hunter Arch. Index.

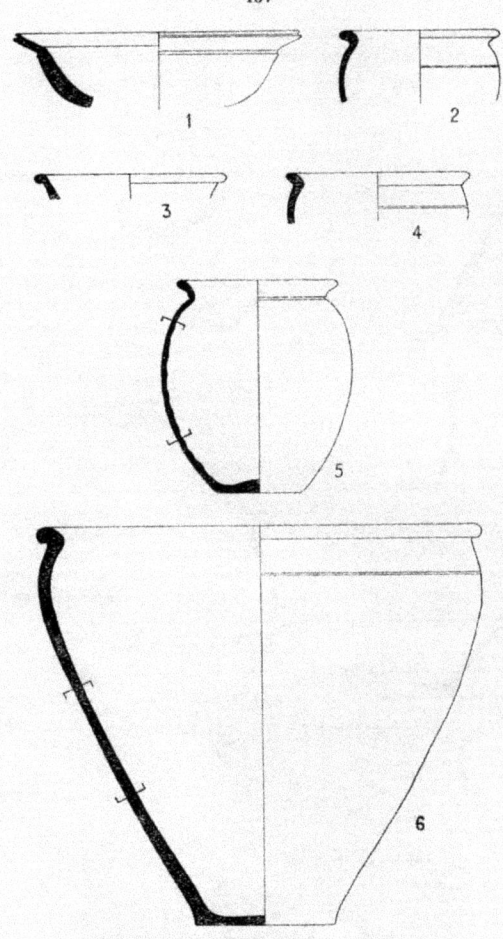

FIG. 3. Scale $\frac{1}{8}$. Brackets indicate restored parts.

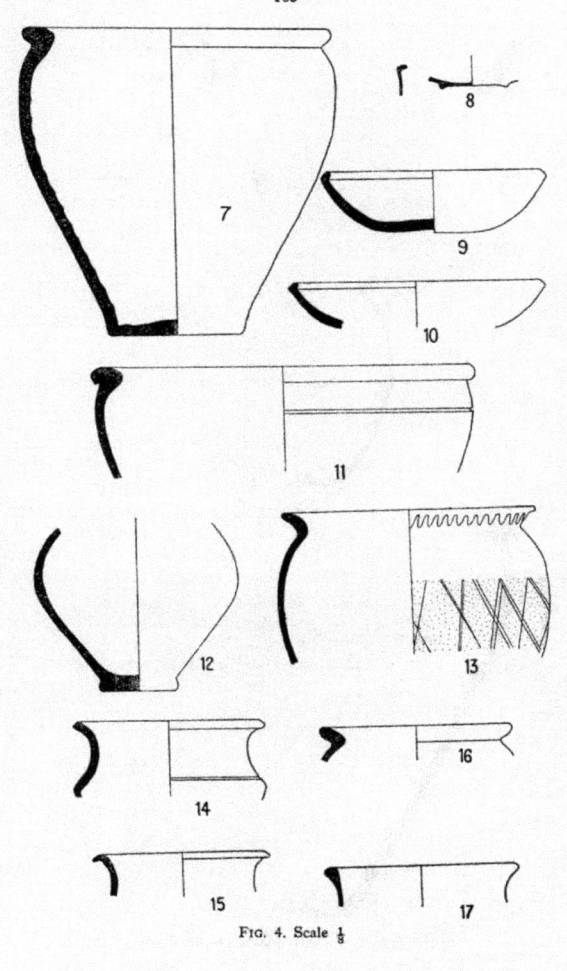

Fig. 4. Scale 1/8

and Faustina),[31] Broomhead (Hadrian),[32] and Oughtibridge, where 5 coins (Vespasian, Domitian, Trajan) probably come from a hoard.[33] Reports of finds in Roman Slack, are substantiated by coins of Vitellius and Orbiana in the Lower Ewden Valley.[34]

Little is known of any settlement which may have flourished around the fort at Templeborough but scattered finds have been recorded in Rotherham. Sherds have been found at Hill Top, Kimberworth,[35] Middle Lane South,[36] and 1st and 2nd century sherds from Canklow Hill.[37] Hoards of coins have been found at Greasborough (3 Postumus, one each of Gordian, Gallus, Victorinus, Claudius Gothicus, Tetricus I, Tetricus II, and Probus),[38] Eldon Road (3rd century coins)[39] and Rotherham Technical College (16 coins including Constans, Magnentius, and Julian II).[40] Isolated coins have been found at Alpha Place (Lucius Verus),[41] Hollowgate Terrace (Constantius II),[42] The Museum (Claudius Gothicus),[43] and Reresby Road (Arcadius).[44]

East of Rotherham, a single sherd has been found of a bowl in hard grey fabric in 1959 by Long Lane, Treeton,[45] and other sherds are known from near Burnt Wood[46] and Hail Mary Hill[47] nearby. A coin hoard was found in 1826 on Guilthwaite Common (1600 coins, mostly Constantine),[48] and isolated coins have been found at Bramley (Aurelian),[49] Maltby (Antonius Pius, Clodius Albinus, Constantine II),[50] Woodhouse (Victorinus),[51] Ulley (Domitian),[52] and Killamarsh (Constantius Chlorus).[53]

Until recently there has been little field work done on the Magnesian Limestone, and wherever detailed field-walking has taken place finds have resulted. At Whitwell (SK543793) 1st to 4th century sherds have been found around a broad hollow,[54] and at Carlton-in-Lindrick (Notts.) Samian and

31 *D.A.J.* 1912, 31.
32 Wilson MS., Sheffield City Library. Coins are said to have been found near Bailey Hill, Bradfield. J. Hunter, Hallamshire, 1869, 461.
33 *T.H.A.S.* IV, 1932, 176.
34 Guest op. cit. 608. *Y.A.J.* XXXVII, 527; *Hunter Arch Index;* coin of Domitian said to be from Bolsterstone.
35 *T.H.A.S.* VII, 21.
36 *Y.A.J.* XXXV, 426.
37 *T.H.A.S.* VI, 191, 260-7. A Samian pot-mould for a medallion of Diana was found at Alma Road in 1894. Whereabouts unknown. W. T. Freemantle, Templeborough 1913, 119.
38 Rotherham Museum.
39 *Y.A.J.* XXXVIII, 528.
40 *Y.A.J.* XXXVIII, 527.
41 *Y.A.J.* XXXV, 225.
42 *Hunter Arch. Index.*
43 *Hunter Arch Index.*
44 *Y.A.J.* XXXVIII, 557.
45 per P. Mellars.
46 *Hunter Arch. Index.*
47 per P. Mellars.
48 Hunter, J., 1831, South Yorkshire, 2, 181.
49 *Y.A.J.* XXXV, 225.
50 *Y.A.J.* XXXV, 95; *C.B.A.* Ann. Rept., 1958, 44.
51 per J. Radley.
52 *Y.A.J.* XXXVII, 528.
53 *E.M.A.B.* 1960, 1.
54 *E.M.A.B.* 1960, 2.

coarse wares were found with iron slag, coal and charcoal when foundations for a bungalow were made (SK 583848).[55] Several sherds of Derbyshire ware have been found above Anston Crags,[56] and coarse wares, including black-burnished fabrics have been found at Hell Wood, Maltby (SK 543906).[57] Ash Tree Cave and all four caves at Creswell have yielded Romano-British pottery—grey wares, black-burnished wares, Castor ware, and calcite-gritted fabric, and Mother Grundy's Parlour has recently produced a corroded coin and a fibula.[58] At Elmton, a rock shelter has yielded a few Roman sherds,[59] and east of Whaley Hall (SK 513713) several hundred sherds have been recovered from what must have been a farmstead during the 2nd and 3rd centuries, yielding grey wares, Samian, and Derbyshire and Dales.[60] At Scratta Wood (SK 543798) an enclosure has an oval perimeter wall with internal sub-divisions and remains of huts, one 16′ in diameter; storage pits and surface levels have yielded good Roman pottery and fibulae of the 2nd and 3rd century, and crude dark native wares which may extend back into the Iron Age. Cattle teeth, bones and saddle querns have also been found.[61] No villa remains are known.

The same area has yielded 3 coin hoards. At Throapham in 1864 two brown-red vases held 1500-2000 coins of Valerian to Aurelius.[62] At North Anston a hoard of 16 silver coins was immediately dispersed, but included coins from Otho to Antoninus Pius,[63] and at Langwith in 1876 a hoard of about 2,000 coins ranged from Valerian to Aurelian.[64] Single coins have been found at Whitwell (Trajan),[65] Dinnington (Claudius Gothicus),[66] Thorpe Salvin (Hadrian).[67]

CONCLUSION

This area, about 150 square miles, set quite close to the main north-south Roman roads, appears to have been a backwater throughout Roman times. There appears to have been a series of occupation sites, some of which may represent small farmsteads where cereals were grown, and pigs, cattle, and sheep were kept, with supplementary food from red and roe deer. There is no evidence of any villages or any villas, but the coin hoards indicate a certain amount of wealth circulating in the area. The material remains summarised above also pose the question: where is the evidence

55 E.M.A.B, 1962, 21.
56 per A. Miller, R. Carr.
57 Y.A.J. XXXV, 95.
58 B.M., Manchester Museum; D.A.J. LXXX, 132-3.
59 per Mrs. Shacklock, Whaley Hall.
60 J. Radley, D.A.J., forthcoming.
61 Scratta Wood, 1959-65: Worksop Arch. Soc. Rept., E.M.A.B., 1960, 10; 1961, 15.
62 Reliq. XXV, 173.
63 Reliq. XXV, 215.
64 Reliq. XXV, 173.
65 E.M.A.B., 1962, 7.
66 Y.A.J. XLI, 5.
67 Y.A.J. XXXVIII, 121. Coins of Claudius, Vespasian and Severus, are said to have come from near Norwood Quarry, Harthill. H. Garbett, History of Harthill, 1950, 15.

for the predecessors of the local Romano-British population? Undoubtedly, the steady recording of small finds and persistent field work will shed more light on this in the next few years.

There is no evidence of any industrial development and only the pottery lends itself to any real analysis. Most significant is the rarity, but not complete absence, of the better pottery such as Samian and later Castor wares. In general, pottery appears to be mainly grey ware, presumably mostly from Cantley, with darker sandy wares and calcite-gritted wares on some sites. Gillam has suggested[68] that Dales Ware and Derbyshire Ware could be expected to be mutually exclusive in distribution, since they have the same function mainly as cooking pots, but a little evidence has been found in the area for both wares occurring on the same site. While Dales Ware is distinctly rarer than Derbyshire Ware, they occur together at Fulwood, Whaley, and South Anston.

Recently, the writers have discovered a small group of fields and enclosures at Smarson Hill Wood, South Anston, which promises to be the most helpful site found up to date in the area for illustrating the native economy in the Sheffield area.[69]

INVENTORY OF POTTERY TYPES FROM KIVETON PARK

1. A fairly rare bowl, 9.1″ across, with thick sides and broad rim with grooved edge standing off the body of the bowl at a sharp angle. The fabric is hard grey and sandy. Occurs at Slack, Pl. xxiv, Nos. 85-9, page 65; Ilkley, Pl. xxxi, No. 25; cf. Gillam 301, and dated to 80-130 A.D.

2. Parts of 3 small jars. The one drawn is 5″ across the rim which is a simple form. The fabric is hard, fine, light grey throughout, and made from a well wedged micaceous clay.

3. A bowl, 6⅝″ across the rim, made of a hard light grey, sandy fabric with a few large quartz inclusions.

4. A small jar with thin (4 mm.) sides and a simple everted rim. Hard, light grey, sandy fabric.

5. A small jar, 5″ across at the rim, 7″ tall, with thin walls (5 mm.), with a rim coming quite sharply off the body. The jar has a hard, pale grey, sandy fabric.

6. A jar, 14″ across the rim, 12½″ high, with a plain roll rim which is quite thick on its inner edge like (7). Fabric hard, grey, and sandy.

7. A slightly lopsided jar, 9.7″ across the rim, 10.1″ high, with a simple roll rim thickened on the inner edge. The fabric is a dark well fired

68 Gillam, J. P., Ant.J., XXXI, 162.
69 T.H.A.S., forthcoming.

clay with large calcite grits which still preserve their identity. So called "native" ware.

8. A small jar with a foot-ring and simple everted rim. The core is a fine hard dense black fabric with a sandy orange slip. Flavian-Trajanic.

9. A deep platter 7" across with inturned rim. The fabric is a hard grey sandy ware with a black burnished surface. Found near the top of the fire pit. 70-100 A.D.

10. A shallow platter 8" across with inturned rim and rising base. A Gallo-Belgic imitation with soapy grey fabric and black burnished surface, dated to 70-100 A.D. From bottom of fire pit and very pocked from over-heating. Cf. Gillam 337; Slack, pl. xxiv, nos. 107-8; Ilkley, pl. xxx, no. 7. Also from Doncaster, in Doncaster Museum.

11. A jar similar to (7), 12" across the rim. The calcite appears to be leached away on the interior face, leaving numerous holes, but is not leached away anywhere on the exterior. This suggests that when being fired the pot was inverted and the inside was heated sufficiently to convert the calcite into lime.

12. The body and base probably of the same flagon, represented by 21 fragments. The base is thick with a groove near the perimeter. It is made of a fine cream paste. Cf. Gillam 3.

13. A tall jar, $6\frac{1}{2}$" across the large simple rim and with exceptionally thin (4 mm.) sides. It has a hard sandy black fabric, with a black burnished surface. A central zone round the body has been left rough and has an irregular lattic decoration. The exterior of the rim has an irregular wavy line which is found only on early jars of this type, c. 120 A.D. Another has lattice of a more regular form. A base related perhaps to a black burnished jar has a stamp on its inner face, which is illegible. Cf. Slack, pl. xxiii, nos. 1-4.

14. A carinated bowl, 6" across the lip with a large everted rim or neck. It has a hard grey sandy fabric with a black-burnished surface. Before 125 A.D. A base with a foot-ring may be related to this vessel.

15. A standard black-burnished jar. It has a brown fabric under a rough black surface. Two other similar jars are represented.

16. A vessel with a long everted neck or rim, carinated with a well-made foot. It is made of a smooth hard grey micaceous clay. Flavian-Trajanic, perhaps like Gillam (77), a carinated beaker.

17. A jar with a simple club rim. The fabric is hard grey and sandy with large chalky inclusions (up to 7 mm.).

Acknowledgment: The writers would like to thank the Hunter Archæological Society for permitting the use of the Archæological Index.

An Unknown Archaeological Site Discovered In Harthill

Since 1987 when I first moved to Harthill, I have been convinced that Hunger Hill on Thorpe Road, Harthill was the site of a hillfort.

In 1998, the landowner allowed me to carry out a field walk up the edge of the field. I found a couple of pieces of small pottery but nothing of any substance. I was told by an archaeologist friend that one piece was Roman.

Later that year I flew over Hunger Hill to take photographs after a dry spell showed up some interesting crop marks. However, a look at an 1851 map of Harthill showed that the crop marks were just the result of hedgerow removal.

Despite not finding any conclusive evidence since 1987, I still felt certain that Hunger Hill was the site of a hillfort and I have carried out research, looked at maps and aerial photographs over the years to prove my hypothesis.

In 2017 new aerial photographs by Google Maps finally provided me with the proof that I had been looking for for 30 years. I contacted the South Yorkshire Archaeological Service to ask if they had any record of any archaeology on Hunger Hill, Harthill. SYAS informed me that they had no record at all of any archaeology at Hunger Hill, Harthill.

This previously unknown and unrecorded site that I have discovered at Harthill, Rotherham looks like it could be an

Iron Age site with a Romano-British site directly over it. It is impossible to say for certain without a proper archaeological investigation of the site being undertaken. Part of the archaeology extends into the adjoining private wood so hopefully, there will be some good archaeological finds in the wood. Below is a photograph of the site.

This site, along with the site I found on Common Road, Harthill in 2005 is among 7 different settlement sites that I believe I have identified within the Harthill with Woodall parish boundary. My evidence shows that there has been continual human occupation at Harthill spanning eleven and a half thousand years.

Sadly, for some unknown reason, aerial LIDAR coverage of the local area stops at the neighbouring village of Whitwell, Derbyshire then leap frogs Harthill and continues at Dinnington. (Correct as of May 2017). When I enquired why this was, the LIDAR archaeologist could not provide me with an explanation, but said it would probably be undertaken at a future date.

My discussions with SYAS have been friendly overall, but they have been generally dismissive and disinterested. The sites that I pointed out to them, and to the Rotherham Planning Committee in 2005 have still not been recorded in their files or investigated further as of May 2017.

From an archaeological point of view Harthill has been totally overlooked, unexplored and ignored. There has never been a professional archaeological dig in Harthill except on new house developments. This makes Harthill unique and special within the UK.

It also provides archaeologists with a unique opportunity to research a site in the UK that has the potential for lots of undisturbed evidence of continual human occupation on one village site spanning eleven and a half thousand years! The possibility of finding plenty of undisturbed archaeological evidence in the fields around the village of Harthill must be huge. I have found lots of archaeological evidence myself just walking along footpaths and field boundaries. They have all been picked up, not dug up or found using a metal detector.

Harthill parish boundary is approximately 1.5 miles wide and 2.5 miles long at its widest points. If I am correct in my belief that I have found seven different settlement sites within the parish boundary of Harthill with Woodall, then this small corner of Rotherham on the South Yorkshire/North Derbyshire county boundary needs to be protected and preserved and explored in detail.

If the Rotherham Borough Council did decide to preserve Harthill village and the countryside around Harthill as a heritage site, then local people could find jobs here in tourism, heritage, education and other ancillary jobs for generations to come which would also bring money into the local Rotherham economy.

I hope that the Rotherham Metropolitan Borough Council will choose to preserve and protect this small corner of Rotherham for future generations, however I doubt that they will. The creeping industrialization from the wind farm development that they sanctioned in 2005 opened the back door to further industrialization of the countryside which is now threatened by greedy corporations wanting to build fracking wells here. This means that the designation of the Green Belt which Harthill sits in, and the RMBC's own designation that Harthill is an "Area of High Landscape Value" is farcical and will quickly lead to the destruction of this unique and special place within the borough of Rotherham.

The wild deer that can often be seen in the fields around the village and all of the different birds and other forms of wildlife that one often sees whilst out walking could soon become nothing more than a distant memory. The quiet country lanes such as Packman Lane which currently measures only 9 feet wide will be widened and the 700 year old hedgerows will be removed and concrete will replace fields which have been farmed for centuries.

If fracking is allowed to go ahead at Harthill, toxic chemicals will be pumped into the ground and possibly even nuclear waste! These poisons will remain in the ground forever. What a sad legacy to leave our children and our grandchildren.

254